YOUR GUIDE TO EATING PLANT FOODS THAT FIGHT DISEASE

BODY ON FIRE

ANTI-INFLAMMATORY COOKBOOK

T0352946

PRAISE FOR

BODY ON FIRE

"Cardiologist, Dr. Monica Aggarwal and Internist, Dr. Jyothi Rao have written an informative book about the importance of inflammation as a trigger for chronic illness. They talk about how to reduce those triggers with lifestyle changes. They emphasize that nutrition is a powerful tool in healing the body; as is sleep, optimism, exercise, and stress reduction. Dr. Aggarwal's personal journey with illness is a backdrop for these changes. I highly recommend this book to everyone who wants to be empowered to be healthy and live a long, full life."

DEAN ORNISH, M.D.
Founder & President, Preventive Medicine Research Institute
Clinical Professor of Medicine, University of California, San Francisco
author, *UnDo It!*

"Drs. Monica Aggarwal and Jyothi Rao's book is the reference text for many decades of a life free of disease. They define in depth the essential components of nutrition, the microbiome, hydration, mental tranquility, sleep, exercise, and more. This book will guide you past each pivot point towards enduring wellness."

CALDWELL B. ESSELSTYN, JR, MD
author of New York Times best-seller *Prevent* and *Reverse Heart Disease*

"A wonderful book! If you want to capture the best from your mind, follow this fantastic guide about how to treat your body."

BARBARA OAKLEY, PHD
Author New York Times science best-seller *A Mind for Numbers*

BODY ON FIRE

ANTI-INFLAMMATORY COOKBOOK

YOUR GUIDE TO EATING PLANT FOODS THAT FIGHT DISEASE

Monica Aggarwal, MD · Jyothi Rao, MD

Book Publishing Company

Summertown, Tennessee

Library of Congress Cataloging-in-Publication Data available upon request.

© 2022 by Monica Aggarwal, MD, and Jyothi Rao, MD

All rights reserved. No portion of this book may be reproduced by any means whatsoever, except for brief quotations in reviews, without written permission from the publisher.

Food photography: Alan Roettinger
Cover photos: Alan Roettinger
Stock photography: 123 RF
Cover and interior design: John Wincek

Printed in the United States of America

BPC
PO Box 99
Summertown, TN 38483
888-260-8458
bookpubco.com

ISBN: 978-1-57067-407-5

Disclaimer: The information in this book is presented for educational purposes only. It isn't intended to be a substitute for the medical advice of a physician, dietitian, or other health-care professional.

Contents

Foreword

You have one life and one body. It is essential to make decisions that keep that body healthy throughout your lifetime. When you were young, you may have believed that you were invincible and that your body could handle anything. As a result, you may have been reckless with your choices, and your body suffered as a result. Today, more than ever before, there is a great deal of pressure to be good at everything you attempt. Consequently, you could end up sacrificing sleep, exercise, and tranquility, and you might make poor choices about what you put into your body. Perhaps you have demanded so much from your body without giving it sufficient time to recover that it has essentially fallen apart—not because it is weak but rather because it is broken.

Monica Aggarwal, MD, experienced this brokenness when she was a young full-time cardiologist, wife, and mother of three children under the age of four. She became sick with a debilitating autoimmune condition.

When the doctor becomes the patient, she changes. She learns how to be a better physician, discovers what patients really need from their doctors, and realizes that patients often leave their doctor's office without getting what they need. She learns how easy it is for doctors to prescribe medications, and how those same medications can make patients feel like hell. She learns about mortality, compassion, vulnerability, and imperfection. A catharsis of sorts, illness became Dr. Aggarwal's savior, because it was through illness that she learned how to truly heal her patients.

Coauthor Jyothi Rao, MD, was frustrated with prescribing countless medications that were nothing more than a way to mask symptoms. The drugs never spoke to true healing. She gave up her traditional practice in internal medicine and started one in integrative medicine instead. She has never looked back.

Together, we had countless discussions about the other side of healing—the one beyond medications. Our common goal has been to empower people to heal themselves by eating wholesome foods with anti-inflammatory spices, using movement and stress-reduction techniques, getting restorative sleep, having a positive outlook, and incorporating many other self-healing approaches.

We wrote *Body on Fire* as a resource for people who are seeking tools to heal themselves—tools that can be used instead of or in addition to medications. We wanted to offer these tools to patients so they could be in the driver's seat and have more control over their health. We came up with the title for the book because it accurately and concisely describes inflammation. The road to healing isn't always easy, but it is definitely worth following. We both walk this path alongside traditional medicine and are pleased to offer options other than pharmaceuticals that can help patients heal. We are thankful every day to be healthy, strong, and free of illness.

Many readers of *Body on Fire* have told us that they love the book but need more guidance on how to get started and what steps to take next. Many people asked for recipes, while others asked for more explanation about how specific foods could benefit them. We set out to write this companion volume to reiterate essential concepts from the main book, offer insight into why certain foods are health-supporting, and provide a how-to-start manual with an abundance of recipes.

Broadly speaking, people get sick because of inflammation, which is essentially the body's response to the stresses placed on it. Inflammation allows illness to grow, which is why this book focuses on calming inflammation. We hope that you enjoy using it as a companion to *Body on Fire* as much as we enjoyed writing it.

Don't try to accomplish all your goals in one day. Change takes time. But don't be afraid to use the tools you have to heal. Take the word *can't* out of your vocabulary. Ask yourself if some habits are worth giving up so you can have more energy, be free of joint pain, walk without chest pain, get off a few or all of your medications, and be happier with your life. We hope your answer is unequivocally yes.

Accept what your body has to give and push it just a bit further. Know that you can do this. Know that we are with you. Be well.

Understanding Inflammation

Inflammation is the body's response to injury. The injury could be from a physical assault or be triggered by an "intruder" (such as a virus or bacteria). The job of the immune system is to recognize which cells are intrinsic and which are foreign. When an unwanted intruder enters the body, the body responds by sending out "insult responders" to heal the damage from the assault. The first responders are the white blood cells, which help target, engulf, and remove the invading culprit and signal and recruit other cells to join the fight. In the process, blood vessels dilate, allowing for greater access to the infected area. Once the culprit is contained, other white blood cells emerge to turn off the body's response. When the first responders have finished their job, the other white blood cells in the body's adaptive immunity step in to create a memory that aids in activating a quick response if the insult should appear again. A strong immune system allows the body to combat these insults.

Problems occur when the immune system battles the same intruder over and over. The continual immune response results in chronic inflammation, which means the immune system is constantly on alert and continually producing insult responders. These responders repeatedly produce signaling molecules to recruit more responders and produce artillery to attack, resulting in inflammatory markers. The markers either stay localized or spread throughout the body, instigating systemic inflammation.

Chronic stressors on the body increase inflammation, giving rise to problems such as weight gain, especially in the midsection, leading to visceral fat and obesity. Visceral fat is highly inflammatory and sends nonstop alarms to the immune system, signaling that the body is on fire. Chronic inflammation can manifest as fatigue, decreased concentration, anxiety, depression, joint pain, digestive problems, or hormone imbalances. Often patients simply don't feel well and have a multitude of symptoms, but their blood work indicates no obvious problems, preventing a clear diagnosis. These patients may be prescribed medication to treat one symptom or another without ever getting to their fundamental issue. The end result is increased inflammation and a greater risk of developing diabetes, autoimmune disease, heart disease, hypertension, and other illnesses.

But hope is not lost. When you listen to your body and make different lifestyle choices, you can decrease inflammation and bring your system back into balance. Good health is within reach!

TWO TYPES OF STRESS

The word *stress* was coined by Hans Seyle, MD, a pioneer in the field of endocrinology. He defined it as the body's demand for change. Stress can be emotional, psychological, physical, chemical, or environmental. Either way, stress ignites a specific reaction in the body, resulting in adaptations that allow it to cope and respond appropriately.

Dr. Seyle defined two types of stress: eustress (stress that has a positive impact on us) and distress (stress that has a negative impact on us). Eustress is driven by positive anticipation, such as expecting a child, receiving a promotion, or going on a vacation. It teaches us coping skills and makes our senses hyperacute. Eustress makes us feel motivated and focused and gives us a positive outlook. Distress, on the other hand, is stress that can have a negative impact on us, such as deadlines, financial problems, or relationship issues. Distress makes us feel unmotivated, tired, and sleepless, and creates digestion issues. Distress can increase oxidative stress and trigger inflammation in the body.

Both eustress and distress are adaptive responses that invoke the autonomic nervous system, which controls involuntary body functions such as heartbeat, body temperature, blood pressure, and digestion. The autonomic nervous system comprises two antagonistic sets of nerves: the sympathetic (fight or flight) and the parasympathetic (rest and digest) nervous systems. They communicate with the brain through chemicals called neurotransmitters that set off a chain of responses affecting different organs and body systems.

During an acute event, the sympathetic nervous system (SNS) is activated, and the body's stress response releases adrenaline to deal with the insult. Adrenaline raises heart rate and blood pressure and increases the production of cortisol, a stress hormone. In a life-threatening event, such as running from a building on fire, cortisol heightens vigilance, sends more blood to the extremities, and dilates the pupils. Cortisol increases glucose in the body so the brain has fuel. It also stores fat in the midsection for future use and acts as an anti-inflammatory during an acute event so you don't feel pain if you are running.

At the same time, the parasympathetic nervous system (PNS) shuts down so the body can focus on survival. It halts digestion, the need for rest, and reproductive urges until you are out of danger. Once the danger is resolved, the PNS is reactivated. Blood pressure and heart rate return to normal levels, digestion restarts, and you are able to relax. You can also feel pain again so you can tend to your wounds. Bladder and bowel functions resume so that toxins can be cleared out of the body. Just like the acute immune response, the sympathetic nervous system can help get you out of danger. But what if you experience stress on a regular basis?

Nowadays, stressors are not necessarily life-threatening, but they may be unrelenting and result in long periods of distress. Chronic distress results in chronic SNS activation, called sympathetic overdrive. When our sympathetic nervous system fires continuously, it triggers significant oxidative stress, resulting in persistent rapid heart rate, increased blood pressure, and elevated cortisol, all of which can weaken the immune system and trigger inflammation.

These stressors sound overwhelming, but the truth is, there is much that's in your control. You can make lifestyle choices that support the parasympathetic nervous system, bring your body back into balance, decrease inflammation, improve your symptoms, and even reverse or prevent illness. *Recognizing what you can control is a huge first step.* You can control how you respond to stressors. You can work on reducing anxiety and worry using mind/body techniques such as yoga, meditation, and breathing exercises. You can prioritize restorative sleep, which allows the body and the immune system to recharge. You can add daily movement with exercise to your routine and use sit-stand desks to minimize sedentary behavior. You can remember to have gratitude and optimism. These practices will aid the PNS and allow for recovery and reduction of distress. They decrease inflammation and help us feel more peaceful and balanced. By decreasing inflammation, we can reduce the triggers for and minimize the impact of chronic illness.

NO MAGIC PILL

Health problems in developed countries are typically addressed with pills. There's a pill for blood pressure, a pill for controlling blood sugar, and even a pill for low moods. These pills may do the job, but they work on a single pathway, a single illness, and can result in undesirable side effects. There are so many other tools, for example, sleep, yoga, optimism, meditation, and exercise, that can reduce stress on the body and suppress inflammation before it has a chance to do permanent damage. Many illnesses, such as immune system disorders, insulin dysregulation, vascular irritation, hormone irregularity, and changes in the gut microbiome, are caused by breakdowns in common pathways, which lead to increased inflammation.

Inflammation can present in different ways in different people, with each person exhibiting specific symptoms or illnesses. But we all can realize broad positive changes by focusing on the root cause of inflammation, identifying and treating the dysfunctional pathways, and making lifestyle modifications. Each lifestyle change can affect several dysfunctions at the same time, unlike a pill that works only on one specific symptom of one specific illness. That pill may treat the illness, but it also might cause negative side effects that could increase the risk of another illness. For instance, treating heart disease with blood thinners can cause the stomach to bleed.

Cleaning up your diet is one of the most important tools you have to reduce inflammation. Cutting out unhealthy foods and adding whole grains, legumes, fruits, vegetables, nuts, and seeds can lower blood pressure, aid weight loss, stabilize blood sugar, increase energy, and make you feel great. Dietary changes also alter the bacteria (microbiota) in the gut microbiome, which is a key part of reducing inflammation. That's because these bacteria are actively involved in the body's immune response to foreign invaders.

EPIGENETICS TO THE RESCUE

Your genes determine whether you will be tall or short or have brown hair or blond. Epigenetics is the study of changes in gene function that do not involve alterations in DNA sequencing. In other words, the concept is that behaviors and the environment can modify how a person's genes work or how they are expressed.

When you make adjustments to your lifestyle (such as your activity level, hours of sleep, degree of stress, and diet), epigenetic changes can occur that in turn influence how your body reads and reacts to genetic sequencing. While these epigenetic changes can't alter your heritable genes, they can change how your body responds to those genes.

Consider Dr. Aggarwal. She developed rheumatoid arthritis because of her genetic sequencing. Her lifestyle at the time she was diagnosed affected how her body reacted to the DNA sequence. She changed her diet, reduced stress, and made other behavioral adjustments. These changes are what healed her. She could not alter her genes, but she could alter her behavior and in turn her epigenetics—the milieu surrounding her genes.

You can have genetic abnormalities—everyone does. But your behavior affects how your body responds to them. Focusing on sleep, movement, what you put into your body, and how you calm your mind are all important. You can change the course of your health!

2 Managing Inflammation with Food

When we address the root cause of an illness, symptoms improve and illness regresses. Addressing the root cause of illness gives you control over your health destiny. Consider what you eat. The wrong foods have poor nutrient quality and excess calories. They also may contain chemical additives, large amounts of salt, added sugar, and saturated fats that can irritate blood vessels, adversely alter the gut microbiome, and spike insulin. All of this can result in fatigue, irritability, anxiety, elevated blood pressure, and bowel irritation, and create an environment conducive to prediabetes. The next thing you know, you have been prescribed a pill for each of these symptoms.

People tend to use food for comfort, to relieve boredom, to connect socially, and to get a dopamine rush that will temporarily elevate their mood. Why does food have this effect? The gut is thought to be our second brain. Jay Pasricha, a physician at Johns Hopkins Hospital, identified the enteric nervous system as a primary communicator to the brain. The gut-brain connection allows communication between the brain and the gut microbiome. The communication is bidirectional, which means that the food you eat affects your brain, and what goes on in your brain affects your gut. For example, eating a lot of pasta might make you feel tired and lethargic, or when you feel sad or anxious, you might get an upset stomach, experience diarrhea, or crave sugar.

It is important to nurture both the brain and the microbiome. The brain is nurtured by sleep and stress-reduction techniques, such as yoga, meditation, and healthy eating. You can help support your microbiome by creating a diverse community of bacteria that affects the way your body breaks down food. Start by eliminating nonnutritious foods and switching to a high-nutrient, plant-based, whole-foods plan. By implementing these simple dietary changes, you can eliminate most or all of the symptoms of disease and, in some cases, even reverse the condition. By combining dietary changes with an assessment of what compels you to choose unhealthy options, you can get to the root causes of illnesses that affect the mind and body.

ANTI-INFLAMMATORY FOODS

If you want to know which foods decrease inflammation, study the list below. Each food is important for a variety of reasons. And these are just *some* of the anti-inflammatory foods available! You can't go wrong by eating a diverse plant-based diet that contains plenty of fiber.

- Almonds
- Avocados
- Beans
- Beets
- Berries
- Broccoli and other cruciferous vegetables
- Cardamom, ground
- Chia seeds
- Chiles
- Cinnamon, ground
- Citrus fruits
- Cherries
- Chocolate, dark (*at least 70 percent cacao*)
- Cloves, ground
- Cocoa (*dairy-free, sugar-free*)
- Flaxseeds, ground
- Garlic
- Ginger
- Green leafy vegetables
- Green tea
- Hemp seeds
- Lentils
- Mushrooms
- Olives
- Orange fruits and vegetables
- Peppers
- Pomegranates
- Probiotic foods (*see page 10*)
- Red grapes
- Tomatoes
- Turmeric
- Walnuts

LONGEVITY

There is nothing you can do to prevent aging. After all, you can't stay twenty forever! But is that really your goal? Or is your goal instead to grow older with strength, grace, and independence, while looking fabulous and feeling fit? The following are keys to longevity:

- Community
- Exercise and movement
- Fasting
- Healthy eating
- Love and friendship
  (*nurturing relationships*)
- Laughter
- Minimal stress
- Optimism
- A sense of purpose
- Sleep

TELOMERES

Everyone has specific goals in life, but in order to achieve those goals, it's essential to maintain core health. One of the reasons some people eat better, sleep better, and look better has to do with their telomere length. Telomeres live at the end of chromosomes (the DNA houses), and they protect the chromosomes from damage. Some people call them the guardians of aging.

When cells divide, the telomeres divide too, and when they divide, the telomeres get shorter. The length of the telomere tells the cells how old they are. As telomeres shorten and age, they divide less frequently, leading to less protection from oxidative damage for the genes. As protection decreases, the risk of chronic illness increases, which can accelerate aging. How much the length of telomeres shorten is determined by genetic and nongenetic factors. Although you can't change the genetic causes, you *can* work on the nongenetic causes.

The key to longevity is to maintain maximum telomere length and minimize shortening. Here's how to grow and stabilize your telomeres:

- Exercise more
- Add sea vegetables to your diet
- Avoid foods with saturated fat
- Drink coffee
- Eat loads of high-fiber foods, such as beans and lentils
- Eat more fruit
- Eat more nuts
- Sleep
- Maintain a healthy weight
- Reduce added sugars from your diet

Here are the habits that shorten telomeres:

- Drinking alcohol
- Being obese
- Eating red meat
- Eating processed meat
- Having a high sugar intake
- Being physically inactive
- Smoking
- Having a sleep deficit

THE MICROBIOME AND ITS MICROBIOTA

The gut microbiota are arguably the body's most important fighters against intruders. The microbiota are the microbes (gut bugs) that are both helpful to the body and potentially harmful. Most are symbiotic (that is, they have a mutually beneficial relationship with the body), but some are pathogenic, which means they promote disease. Pathogenic and symbiotic microbiota usually coexist without problems. However, poor diets (as well as infectious illnesses or the prolonged use of antibiotics or other bacteria-destroying medications) can cause an imbalance known as dysbiosis, making the body more susceptible to disease.

Someone who eats a lot of sugar, simple carbohydrates (see page 20), and red meat will have different microbiota than someone who eats plenty of fruits and vegetables, complex carbohydrates, and no meat. In fact, the microbiota associated with inflammatory illnesses and heart disease are more common in people who eat an unhealthy diet. But people who improve their diets can begin creating healthier microbiota within just six days.

Microorganisms in the microbiome make byproducts known as metabolites, and different microorganisms make different metabolites. When you eat a high-fiber, plant-based diet, bacteria in the microbiome will make anti-inflammatory short-chain fatty acids that help create a strong barrier against invaders. If you eat a low-fiber diet, the body will make fewer short-chain fatty acids, resulting in less anti-inflammatory power. The more fiber you eat, the more anti-inflammatory power you get.

When omnivores eat a piece of red meat, their bodies produce elevated levels of a certain metabolite called trimethylamine N-oxide (TMAO) that is associated with increased heart disease and heart failure. If vegans were to eat a piece of red meat, they would make only minimal amounts of this metabolite. This suggests that meat eaters and vegans have different gut bugs because they make different levels of that metabolite associated with heart disease. There are other metabolites made in the gut as well that are produced with the ingestion of high-fat foods and are associated with chronic illnesses.

The goal is to strengthen the microbiota so you have less inflammation and less chronic illness. You can do that by increasing your intake of high-fiber foods and adding in fermented foods. Here is a good list of foods to strengthen the gut.

- Beans and other legumes
- Complex carbohydrates
- Fruits and vegetables
- Nuts and seeds
- Anti-inflammatory spices
- Fermented foods like kimchi, sauerkraut, and tempeh

You also can greatly decrease your chances of experiencing chronic inflammation and chronic disease by eliminating the following dietary triggers:

- Dairy products
- Fried foods
- Meat, poultry, and seafood
- Packaged and processed foods
- Simple sugars and syrups

Easy, right? No, but necessary. The food you eat has been hurting your body for so long that it has become necessary to make significant changes so you can recover from the inside. If you can heal your gut microbiota/microbiome, you can start to heal your body.

PROBIOTICS AND PREBIOTICS

Probiotics are health-promoting (good) microorganisms that are in fermented foods. They actually have the gut bugs in them. Prebiotics are dietary fibers that can't be digested without the presence of this good bacteria. Prebiotic foods feed the good bacteria so they can produce anti-inflammatory short-chain fatty acids and strengthen the microbiome barrier.

You can take a probiotic supplement, but many brands include bacteria that have questionable benefit. A better option is to get these healthy microorganisms from your foods. Think about how to add probiotics and prebiotic foods to your daily diet.

PROBIOTIC FOODS

- Kimchi
- Miso
- Natto
- Sauerkraut
- Tempeh
- Yogurt

PREBIOTIC FOODS

- Apples
- Asparagus
- Bananas
- Barley
- Beans (all types)
- Chicory root
- Cocoa powder, unsweetened
- Dandelion greens
- Flaxseeds
- Garlic
- Jerusalem artichokes
- Jicama
- Leeks
- Lentils (all types)
- Oats
- Onions
- Sea vegetables
- Wheat bran
- Yacon root

Essential Vitamins and Minerals

VITAMIN B$_{12}$

Vitamin B$_{12}$ promotes the normal functioning of the nervous system and the production of hemoglobin (needed for healthy red blood cells and energy). It also plays a major role in helping the body convert fats and proteins into energy and enhances the immune system's response to disease by fighting off germs and other invasive organisms. Vitamin B$_{12}$ is required for skin, bone, and nail health, but even more important, it is necessary for cognitive function and memory. Patients were found to have less brain fog when they increased their levels of vitamin B$_{12}$. In one study, adding vitamin B$_{12}$ and omega-3 fatty acids to the diets of patients with early dementia appeared to decrease their rate of cognitive decline. Finally, vitamin B$_{12}$ is water soluble, which means that excess amounts are expelled through urination.

Typically, vitamin B$_{12}$ deficiency occurs in older individuals, who generally have less acid in their stomachs, and can be seen in people who follow a vegetarian or vegan diet. Others at risk are those who have had gastrointestinal surgeries, such as gastric bypass, people with inflammatory bowel disease (Crohn's disease or ulcerative colitis), people who take the drug metformin, and those who frequently use proton pump inhibitors. People who eat animal products often use this as a criticism of a plant-based diet. The truth is that vitamin B$_{12}$ is made by bacteria in the soil. Cows that eat the grass and soil used to get enough B$_{12}$ to then supply the humans who ate the cow. However, cows now suffer from cobalt deficiency and therefore can't process vitamin B$_{12}$. Cobalt deficiency is more prevalent because of leached, overused soils. As a result, cows often have to be injected with vitamin B$_{12}$ to keep their levels up. Truly, almost anyone can be at risk for vitamin B_{12} deficiency, which is why levels should be checked regularly, especially later in life.

The human body cannot produce vitamin B_{12}, so we must obtain it from the foods we eat or from supplements. Vitamin B_{12} can be found naturally in some seaweeds and mushrooms. Many foods are now fortified with vitamin B_{12}.

An excellent alternative is to add nutritional yeast flakes (*Saccharomyces cerevisiae*) to your diet. Nutritional yeast is deactivated, meaning that it has no leavening power. Its delicious flavor adds umami to salads, stews, pasta dishes, and vegetables. Look for a brand that is fortified with vitamin B_{12}.

There are many effective vitamin B_{12} supplements that can be purchased over the counter that are safe even for children. The recommended daily allowance of vitamin B_{12} for adults can be found on multiple websites by searching for "RDA vitamin B_{12}."

CALCIUM

Calcium is stored primarily in teeth and bones. It plays an important role in the body's basic mechanisms, such as the communication between nerves and organs, vascular strength (strength of blood vessels), and muscle contractility. How well the body absorbs calcium depends on a person's age and vitamin D levels as well as nutritional factors in their food. Plant-based sources of calcium include the following:

- Almonds
- Blackstrap molasses
- Bok choy
- Broccoli
- Cabbage
- Chia seeds
- Collard greens
- Figs
- Kale
- Okra
- Sesame seeds
- Tofu
- Turnip greens

VITAMIN D

Vitamin D appears to be as important as calcium for bone health. Having low levels of vitamin D has been associated with increased fracture risk. The best way to get vitamin D is through sun exposure. Ten to thirty minutes of midday sun a few days a week is usually sufficient for most individuals, unless they are in a high-risk group. People who have the highest risk of vitamin D deficiency are obese individuals (because fat cells sequester vitamin D), dark-skinned individuals (as they may not absorb this nutrient from the sun very well), people who live at high altitudes, seniors (who have fewer vitamin D precursors in their skin), people with malabsorption (as they are unable to absorb vitamin D and other fats), and people who regularly use sunscreen. Of course, if you are at high risk of skin cancer, sun exposure isn't a good option for you.

Vitamin D is harder than calcium to get from the diet, but it can be done. In general, animal sources provide vitamin D_3 and plant sources provide vitamin D_2, although vitamin D_2 may not be as effective at raising vitamin D levels in the blood. Plant-based vitamin D_3 is obtained from lichen. Most people, regardless of their diet, need to supplement their vitamin D due to spending so much time indoors. Commercial plant-based milks are usually fortified with vitamin D. If you wish to use a supplement, consider taking vitamin D_3, but don't take more than 1,000 to 2,000 IU per day without consulting a physician. Too much vitamin D can be toxic.

Plant-based sources of vitamin D include the following:

- Fortified soy milk
- Fortified almond and other nut milks
- Fortified orange juice
- Wild mushrooms

IRON

Anemia is a common problem, especially for menstruating women. Perimenopausal women are also prone to anemia, as their cycles can become heavier and more irregular. That said, many people simply do not get sufficient iron through diet alone.

However, it is a common misconception that you can't get enough iron through a plant-based diet. The fact is that you can, and it is arguably a healthier version. Iron from animals is heme iron, whereas iron found in plants is non-heme. Heme iron has been associated with increased risk of cardiovascular disease, type 2 diabetes, and certain cancers. Although non-heme iron is more difficult to absorb, it is possible to get a sufficient amount through plant-based foods. And since iron can be pro-oxidant at certain levels, increasing our risk of these illnesses, the lower absorption rate of non-heme iron may actually be beneficial. The following are some readily available foods that are rich in non-heme iron:

- Amaranth
- Black beans
- Blackstrap molasses
- Chickpeas
- Dark chocolate
  (at least 70 percent cacao)
- Dark-green leafy vegetables
- Lentils
- Mung beans
- Navy beans
- Pumpkin seeds
- Quinoa
- Soybeans
- Spelt
- Tofu
- Whole grains

POTASSIUM

Most Americans don't get enough potassium in their diets. Potassium regulates fluid balance, aids in muscle contractions, and sends nerve signals. If you have high blood pressure, eating foods high in potassium will help lower it. The following are some delicious and versatile potassium-rich plant foods:

- Avocados
- Bananas
- Beans
- Cucumbers
- Honeydew melon
- Kale
- Lentils
- Mushrooms
- Oranges
- Peas
- Pumpkins
- Sweet potatoes
- Zucchini

4

Macronutrients

FATS

Fats are essential for good health, but people tend to eat way too much of them. The various types of fats include saturated, unsaturated, and trans fats. Saturated fats tend to make low-density lipoprotein (LDL), the so-called bad cholesterol, go up. They have been associated with heart disease and should be avoided. Saturated fats are primarily found in animal products, such as meat and high-fat dairy products. They can also be found in some plant-based foods, such as avocado, coconut, and nuts, but in much smaller amounts. Studies show that if you switch from saturated to unsaturated fats in your diet, you can reduce your risk of heart disease.

Unsaturated fat is better. Unsaturated fats include monounsaturated fats (found in avocado, olive oil, and many nuts) and polyunsaturated fats (found in corn, safflower, and sunflower oils). There are two main groups of polyunsaturated fats: omega-3 and omega-6 fatty acids. Some data suggests that replacing saturated fats and refined carbohydrates with unsaturated fats and complex carbohydrates will result in lower cholesterol and reduced triglycerides.

However, oil is a concentrated plant-based fat. In general, one tablespoon of oil contains about 14 grams of fat, so it is very dense. There is evidence that many oils cause plaque in the arteries. Flax and canola oils have an omega-6 to omega-3 ratio of 2:1, which is better than other oils.

Extra-virgin olive oil is highly concentrated in fat, much like the other oils. It is about 14 percent saturated fat and 11 percent polyunsaturated fat. Unlike other oils, however, it is higher in monounsaturated fat (72 percent) and anti-oxidants and is rich in polyphenols (plant nutrients), which may give it beneficial properties for overall health and heart health. Even though there are many studies that support this line of thought, there is much to still be understood.

Of all the oils to use, extra-virgin olive oil and avocado oil are probably the most prudent choices, maybe canola oil as well. Flaxseed oil cannot be used in cooking. In our recipes, we focus on using minimal oil in general. If oil is included, we use extra-virgin olive oil in the smallest amount necessary (no more than two teaspoons per serving).

As a rule, less oil is probably better. Your goal should be to eat a primarily plant-based diet with plenty of fruits and vegetables that is high in fiber, low in saturated fats, and includes plenty of anti-inflammatory foods. Whether you eat a little of this or a little of that probably won't matter to a great extent, as long as you eat well the majority of the time.

PROTEIN

Proteins are made from building blocks called amino acids. Proteins make hormones and neurotransmitters, and they form enzymes, which direct most reactions in the body. They have an influence on the immune, endocrine, and musculoskeletal systems, and they also help to grow and repair the body. Unlike carbohydrates and fats, proteins are not a great source of energy.

The proteins in the body are made up of twenty amino acids. All twenty are necessary for optimal nutrition. Many amino acids are "essential," which means they must be obtained from food; the body cannot make them. Amino acids can be found in both animal products and plant-based foods, but diets high in animal proteins are higher in saturated fats and cholesterol, and some fish have been found to have high metal content, such as mercury. In addition, animal sources have higher amounts of heme iron, which has been associated with several cancers, type 2 diabetes, and coronary artery disease. Protein from fish, eggs, and beef increase the level of trimethylamine N-oxide, which is correlated with higher risk of heart disease. Plant-based proteins, on the other hand, are low in saturated fats, high in vitamins and minerals, and rich in fiber, which helps keep the microbiome diverse and balanced. *It is absolutely possible to get sufficient amino acids from a plant-based diet!* In fact, a plant-based diet has been shown to prevent obesity, type 2 diabetes, cardiovascular disease, and some cancers.

A pervasive belief is that when we're tired, it's a sign that we need more protein. The truth is that protein deficiency is a myth. Most people aren't chronically tired because they're protein deficient; they are tired because they eat too much sugar and refined foods. When you stop eating sugar and switch to a whole-foods, plant-based diet, that constant feeling of being tired will soon be a distant memory.

OMEGA-3 AND OMEGA-6 FATTY ACIDS

The human body needs fatty acids, especially omega-3s and omega-6s. Omega-3 fatty acids contain eicosapentaenoic acid (EPA) and docosahexaenoic acid (DHA), which are potent anti-inflammatories that can curb joint stiffness. They are also good for reducing triglycerides. When patients with elevated risk for heart disease are given highly purified EPA (branded as VASCEPA), they have decreased risk of having a serious heart attack or stroke. Fatty acids seem to play a role in attention, cognition, depression, and memory, and are thought to aid brain development in children. Omega-6 fatty acids are also important because they are pro-inflammatory and promote clotting. These fatty acids are needed in times of injury.

The problem is that the typical American diet is loaded with high amounts of omega-6 fatty acids and low amounts of omega-3 fatty acids. The ratio is almost 10:1, so there is an imbalance favoring inflammation, which suggests that we should limit foods that are high in omega-6s and increase foods that are high in omega-3s.

Alpha-linolenic acid (ALA) is a type of omega-3 fatty acid found in plants. ALA does not easily convert to EPA and DHA. However, ALA appears to benefit people with heart disease, high blood pressure, and maybe even high cholesterol, without converting to EPA/DHA. More studies are needed, but ALA seems to be a potent anti-inflammatory on its own.

Ideally, omega-3 fatty acids should be obtained from foods, but supplements are available. Omega-3 supplements are highly unregulated, as are all nutraceuticals. There is a wide range in the amount of EPA and DHA in supplements and there often are many fillers as well. The optimal proportion of EPA and DHA is not clear. Recent studies suggest that EPA is of greater benefit, but more studies are needed.

The following are good plant-based sources of omega-3 fatty acids:

- Brussels sprouts
- Chia seeds
- Flaxseeds
- Hemp seeds
- Walnuts

The following are good plant-based sources of omega-6 fatty acids:

- Hemp seeds
- Sunflower seeds
- Tofu

SHINING A LIGHT ON SOY

People are often confused about soy products. Women may be concerned that soy will increase their risk of breast cancer (it will not). Men may worry that too much soy will cause them to grow breasts (it will not) or develop prostate issues (it will not do that either). Studies do not support the notion of increased breast cancer or any cancer. In fact, traditional soy foods may even lower rates of breast cancer.

Soybeans are a wonderful source of plant protein. They are loaded with phytoestrogens, such as isoflavones, which are anti-inflammatory. There is some data for the benefits of soy on cholesterol as well. Soy is a complete protein, which means it contains all the essential amino acids the body needs.

Soy can be enjoyed in the form of tofu, soymilk, tempeh (fermented soybeans), edamame (green soybeans cooked or boiled in their pods), or dried and cooked soybeans, which are fiber rich. Try to avoid eating foods containing soy protein isolates, such as meat alternatives, as they are highly processed, low in phytoestrogens, and low in fiber.

The recommended daily requirements for protein are available online. Don't worry about the numbers, though, because you are unlikely to experience protein deficiency as long as you eat a balanced plant-based diet. Excellent plant-based protein sources include the following:

- Almonds
- Brazil nuts
- Broccoli
- Cashews
- Chia seeds
- Edamame
- Hemp seeds
- Kale
- Legumes *(beans, lentils, peas)*
- Mycoprotein *(from mushrooms)*
- Pistachios
- Potatoes
- Quinoa
- Seitan
- Spelt
- Spinach
- Spirulina
- Teff
- Tempeh
- Tofu
- Whole wheat flour

THE VALUE OF LECTINS

Lectins are proteins that can bind to carbohydrates. They are stable in acidic environments, which means they do not break down. Lectins are found in all plants, but raw beans, lentils, peas, soybeans, and whole wheat have especially high levels. Some people claim that lectins decrease absorption of minerals—especially calcium, iron, phosphorus, and zinc—and have suggested that lectins cause inflammatory conditions, such as rheumatoid arthritis and type 1 diabetes. These theories have few human-based studies to support their claims.

Dan Buettner is the best-selling author who coined the term *Blue Zone* for places like Okinawa, Sardinia, and parts of Greece that have large numbers of people living into their eighties, nineties, and even older, with low rates of chronic illness. They eat plenty of lectin in those communities because their diets are rich in legumes. Foods high in lectins are a source of antioxidants and provide excellent nourishment for the gut. They reduce spikes in blood sugar by slowing down digestion and the absorption of carbohydrates. Foods with lectins also are good sources of B vitamins, protein, and fiber. These are foods to *keep* in your diet, not remove.

The potential harm from lectins comes from uncooked dried beans. Soaking dried legumes (beans and lentils) for several hours and then boiling or stewing them minimizes the potential risk of eating lectins. Sprouting seeds, nuts, legumes, or grains also dramatically reduces any potential issues with lectins. Another simple method to decrease lectins is simply to remove the hull or the shell of beans or grains. People don't typically eat dried beans, so even thinking about how to deal with lectins is really a nonissue. We strongly recommend eating lectin-rich foods! Don't think about this one too much—eat your beans!

A lot of people say they don't like the texture of beans and lentils, but these foods are very good for you. Beans are highly recommended because they are anti-inflammatory, rich in fiber, high in potassium, and low in insulin activation. They are a win-win! Learn to love them.

Start by adding one serving of legumes to your diet every day. Try different kinds and colors: black beans, kidney beans, navy beans, lentils. If you don't like the texture of cooked beans, blend them into a soup or sauce. Experiment with a variety of recipes to find the ones you like best.

CARBOHYDRATES

eople are often confused about carbohydrates. Are they healthful or damaging? Carbohydrates are macronutrients, just like proteins and fats, and include sugars, fiber, and starches. They are found in breads, beans, dairy products, vegetables, and fruits. Carbohydrates are powerful sources of energy, especially for the brain. And just like protein, there are favorable and unfavorable types.

Carbohydrates can be simple (refined) or complex (unrefined). Simple carbohydrates include sugar and refined grains (such as white rice, white bread, and pasta). Examples of complex carbohydrates are brown rice, quinoa, whole rolled oats, other whole grains, fruits, vegetables, and legumes. Which type of carbohydrate you consume will affect how quickly its sugar gets into your bloodstream. If you are active, the sugar is quickly utilized by the body. If you are not active, the pancreas will produce insulin that turns the sugar into fat. Without this conversion, the sugar would stay in your bloodstream and cause inflammation. The more sugar and sugary foods you eat, and the less active you are, the more insulin will work to produce fat deposits.

Cells have insulin receptors that allow them to take in sugar for processing. When there is more sugar coming into the body, the ability of fat cells to absorb that sugar becomes impaired. At that point, patients become *insulin resistant*, meaning their insulin can't do its job, and sugars float freely in the bloodstream, causing the breakdown of blood vessels and provoking inflammation. We see this a lot in obese patients.

The best thing you can do is decrease the amount of simple sugars you eat and switch to whole foods with complex carbohydrates. Complex carbohydrates are harder to break down and digest, thereby minimizing the activation of insulin. As a bonus, foods with complex carbohydrates help you feel fuller longer, and you get the benefits of the fiber, vitamins, and minerals they contain. You will also start to trim down, and as you trim down, your cells will become less insulin resistant and will be able to more effectively handle the small amount of sugar coming into the body. Say goodbye to prediabetes and maybe even diabetes!

The average person's diet should be 50–55 percent carbohydrates. The key, though, is to eat *complex* carbohydrates, not simple ones. Fruits are considered simple carbohydrates because they have a lot of naturally occurring sugar. But unlike refined carbohydrates, they are loaded with fiber, vitamins, and phytonutrients. So although they are simple carbohydrates, their fiber content makes them more complex.

Carbohydrates are the primary source of energy for the body and should be eaten daily and often. The secret is to eat foods that are as unprocessed as possible. The recipes in this book use very little added sugar except in the

PHYTONUTRIENTS

Phytonutrients are nutrients that come from plants. They can be found in fruits, vegetables, nuts, beans, and tea. Phytonutrients defend the body against illness.

There are over 25,000 phytonutrients available in plants. How they all function is not known. Some important phytonutrients are carotenoids, flavonoids, phytoestrogen, and resveratrol. Each phytonutrient offers an array of benefits, such as keeping blood vessels dilated, maintaining eye health, and lowering cancer risk. As not all fruits and vegetables possess the same phytonutrients, eat foods in a variety of colors to ensure you are getting the health benefits from a wide range of phytonutrients.

TABLE 1. Phytonutrient sources and benefits

PHYTONUTRIENTS	FOOD SOURCES		BENEFITS
Carotenoids (beta-carotene, lutein, lycopene)	bell peppers cantaloupe carrots kale mango	spinach sweet potatoes tomatoes watermelon	antioxidant, boosts immune system, improves eye health lowers risk of cancer, lowers risk of heart disease
Curcumins	turmeric		anti-inflammatory, antioxidant, improves memory, lowers risk of cancer
Ellagic acid	blackberries grapes pomegranate	raspberries strawberries walnuts	antioxidant, improves insulin sensitivity, lowers risk of cancer, reduces blood pressure
Flavonoids (quercetin, flavonols)	apples berries cocoa coffee ginger grapefruit	kale leeks lemons onions tea tomatoes	increases longevity, lowers risk of heart disease, reduces blood pressure
Lignans	apricots broccoli flaxseeds	kale sesame seeds strawberries	lowers risk of cancer, heart disease, and osteoporosis, and reduces menopausal symptoms
Resveratrol	blueberries cocoa cranberries	grapes peanuts red wine	anti-inflammatory, antioxidant, improves insulin sensitivity, increases longevity

dessert section. It's okay to have a treat once in a while. The rest of the time, aim for good, healthy eating. The following are some great sources of complex carbohydrates:

- Barley
- Broccoli (and other vegetables)
- Buckwheat
- Edamame
- Flaxseeds
- Fruits
- Kamut

- Legumes (beans, lentils, peas)
- Millet
- Oats
- Quinoa
- Spelt
- Squashes
- Sweet potatoes

SPICES

Spices are an essential part of a plant-based diet. In addition to their spectacular flavor, spices have many medicinal properties due to their concentrated levels of phytonutrients, which are associated with cell signaling and play a large role in turning off inflammation and lowering oxidative stress in the body. Some phytonutrients can only be found in spices. Try to work spices into your diet every day, at every meal. Experiment with different combinations to experience the vast variety of flavors and aromas they contribute. You can also add spices, such as ground cinnamon and nutmeg, to beverages. Table 2, page 23, shows just a few of the many spices available and some of their primary health benefits.

TABLE 2. Spices and their active ingredients and benefits

SPICE	ACTIVE INGREDIENT(S)	ACTION
Basil	citronellol, eugenol, linalool	antioxidant
Black cumin	thymoquinone	immune booster
Black pepper	piperine	protects brain cells
Cardamon	cineole	anti-inflammatory, antioxidant
Cayenne	capsaicin	pain reliever
Cinnamon	cinnamaldehyde	lowers blood sugar
Cloves	eugenol	pain reliever
Garlic	allicin	blood thinner
Ginger	gingerol	anti-nausea
Mint	menthol	anti-nausea, pain reliever, promotes gut health
Paprika	carotenoids	antioxidant
Rosemary	rosmarinic acid	antioxidant
Star anise	flavonoids	antifungal, antioxidant
Tarragon	carotenoids	anti-inflammatory
Turmeric	curcumin	anti-inflammatory

5

The Effects of Food on Sleep, Exercise, and Outlook

SLEEP

There are many foods that affect sleep. Foods high in the amino acid tryptophan promote sleep. Tryptophan helps produce melatonin, which can regulate sleep cycles, and serotonin, which stabilizes mood. Almonds, walnuts, kiwifruit, and tart cherries are good sources of melatonin.

Magnesium promotes sleep because it helps regulate melatonin. Magnesium binds to gamma-aminobutyric acid receptors. These receptors act as neurotransmitters, which means they transmit information to the brain. In this way, magnesium helps to quiet the brain. Foods high in magnesium include avocados, dark chocolate (at least 70 percent cacao), cocoa (dairy-free, sugar-free), dates, flaxseeds, nuts, legumes, pumpkin seeds, tofu, and sunflower seeds.

Bananas are high in tryptophan, magnesium, and potassium and can help you stay asleep. Starchy foods, such as rice and potatoes, also can increase tryptophan. Kale and spinach are high in magnesium and produce nitric oxide, which is a gas that can lower blood pressure.

An excess of stimulants during the day can disrupt your sleep cycle. Having black or green tea or caffeinated beverages even in the early afternoon can inhibit your ability to fall asleep. Alcohol might seem relaxing, but it can adversely affect your quality of sleep. Eating your last meal of the day three or four hours prior to bedtime will help minimize acid reflux and heartburn overnight. Reduce your fluid intake two hours before bedtime to lessen the chance of waking up during the night to use the bathroom.

The following foods help promote sleep:

- Almonds
- Avocados
- Cherries, tart
- Chocolate, dark
  (*at least 70 percent cacao*)
- Dates
- Flaxseeds
- Kale
- Kiwifruit
- Legumes (*beans, lentils*)
- Potatoes
- Pumpkin seeds
- Rice
- Spinach
- Sunflower seeds
- Tofu
- Walnuts

EXERCISE

Movement and exercise play a large part in both health and sleep. Regular exercise reduces the risk of chronic illnesses, such as cancer, cardiovascular disease, and diabetes, and boosts memory. Movement and exercise elevate mood and promote better rest, which in turn encourages better food choices. A nutrient-rich, lower-calorie diet of whole plant-based foods can boost energy, enhance performance, increase stamina and strength, and decrease recovery time. Eating too much fat or too many pro-inflammatory foods, such as simple carbohydrates, can make you feel sluggish, so focus instead on complex carbohydrates and protein-rich foods.

Foods that help improve performance include the following:

- Amaranth
- Brazil nuts
- Brown rice
- Bulgur
- Cashews
- Chia seeds
- Edamame
- Farro
- Legumes (*beans, lentils, peas*)
- Nut butters
- Oats
- Pumpkin seeds
- Quinoa
- Split peas, green or yellow
- Tempeh
- Tofu
- Walnuts

Hydration is also key to stamina, performance, and recovery. Increase your intake of water during and after workouts. Fruit is a great choice for a post-workout snack. The natural sugar in fruit can restore energy to your muscles and brain. Fiber in fruit helps prevent a drop in blood sugar following a workout. In addition, foods that are high in magnesium and potassium benefit muscles.

For a refreshing drink that restores carbohydrates, protein, and fats and that also contains B-complex vitamins, iron, and magnesium, try a green smoothie made with plant-based milk. Use spinach, kale, or another green leafy vegetable. Then add berries and chia seeds, hemp seeds, or flaxseeds.

Foods that help improve recovery from exercise include the following:

- All foods listed in Table 1, page 21
- Bananas
- Berries, especially blueberries
- Chia seeds
- Dark-green leafy vegetables
- Flaxseeds
- Hemp seeds
- Pears

OUTLOOK

Studies show that a positive outlook can improve not only your health but also your longevity. This may be because optimists experience less stress, thereby reducing the release of cortisol and adrenaline, the hormones involved in the body's fight-or-flight response. Optimists are thought to make better health choices, such as not smoking, and may be more inclined to exercise. They tend to have increased levels of antioxidants in the blood, which may be due to their higher intake of fruits and vegetables, though it's not clear if they are eating a healthier diet because they are optimistic or whether they are optimistic because they are eating a healthier diet. Maybe it's both!

Optimism can be learned using techniques such as daily gratitude journaling. As you work toward making smarter lifestyle choices and being proactive about your health, you will feel more empowered and optimistic about your future.

6

Let's Begin!

Remember that change takes time. During the first six weeks of your new diet, adhere as best you can to the foods recommended in this section. The goal is to calm inflammation and reduce your risk of illness. There are multiple steps involved with healing, but nutrition should be the first one you turn to. After the first six weeks, start adding other options from this recipe book as desired.

When you eat is nearly as important as what you eat. Most people are busy and active between the hours of 7:00 a.m. and 6:00 p.m. In the evening, they do a lot of sitting, watching television, relaxing, and sleeping. The period of the day when you are most active is when you should be eating. When you aren't eating (fasting period), the body stores fat for energy and produces ketones, which seem to benefit endothelial function (the dilation of blood vessels) and decrease inflammation. Eating smaller evening meals and walking after dinner can improve blood sugar levels. The following is an outline of what to put into your body and when.

Breakfast: BETWEEN 6:00 A.M. AND 8:00 A.M.

Begin with taking into account what time you go to sleep and what time you wake up. The average adult should be sleeping seven to nine hours each night. If you go to bed at 10:00 p.m., you should wake up between 5:00 a.m. and 7:00 a.m. Determine your wake-up time based on when you leave for work or when your day starts. Create a morning ritual. Try to have at least one hour at home to calm your mind, go for a short walk (walking on an empty stomach is most effective for losing weight), take a shower, and eat breakfast. Here are a few options for your morning meal:

- Whole wheat bread with oil-free hummus *(see recipe, page 112)*, sliced tomato, black pepper, and sprouts
- Whole wheat bread with avocado
- Hot oatmeal made with whole rolled oats cooked in water and topped with a handful of blueberries *(do not add sweetener of any kind)*
- Muesli *(see recipe, page 35)* served with unsweetened almond milk and fresh fruit or berries
- Water
- A smoothie *(see recipes, pages 36–40)*
- A cup of coffee, ideally black

If you have coffee, there should be no sugars in it. If needed, add a plant-based milk. Teas are also a good option. Green tea is less bitter than black tea. Add ¼ teaspoon of turmeric to your coffee or tea.

WHOLE WHEAT BREAD

Look for bread that is minimally processed and contains only a few ingredients: whole wheat flour, water, yeast, maybe salt. Breads with nuts or seeds added are also good choices. Avoid any that contain sugar, oil, or preservatives.

Most commercial whole wheat breads include other flours in addition to whole wheat, and even organic brands typically contain sugar, molasses, or oil. They may also have mono- and diglycerides, which are preservatives. The deli departments in grocery stores make the components for bread in warehouses, then finish the last step in the store to give the impression that the bread is freshly baked. Seek out local bakeries that make fresh bread, but ask about the ingredients they use. Alternatively, you could try Ezekiel sprouted grain bread, which is made without preservatives; it can be found in the freezer section of most natural food stores.

Snacktime: BETWEEN 10:00 A.M. AND 11:00 A.M.

If you're hungry for a snack, here are some good options:

- One handful of unsalted nuts *(any variety is fine, but almonds and walnuts, which are rich in omega-3 fatty acids, are especially beneficial; measure carefully, as nuts are very easy to overeat)*
- One piece of fresh fruit
- Raw vegetable sticks *(dip in oil-free hummus, if desired)*
- Banana and unsweetened, no-salt-added peanut butter or other nut butter
- Water

Lunch: BETWEEN 12:00 NOON AND 3:00 P.M.

Lunch should be a large salad made primarily with dark-green leafy vegetables, such as kale, spinach, chard, arugula, or escarole. Romaine is a good choice, too, but dark greens are better. Iceberg lettuce has no real nutritional value. The green part of the salad should be larger than your head.

Add any vegetables that you want, such as carrots, cucumbers, broccoli, mushrooms, tomatoes, and so forth. Include cooked or canned chickpeas (rinsed and drained) or other legumes, which contain both complex carbohydrates and protein. Alternatively, add cooked tempeh or raw or baked tofu. (Do not add croutons or any animal products.)

For dressing, use balsamic vinegar and/or oil-free hummus or any of the salad dressing recipes in this book. Sprinkle nutritional yeast flakes over the top, if you like. It will add a delicious flavor, and fortified nutritional yeast is a good source of vitamin B_{12}.

For your first six weeks on this plan, enjoy this salad every day. Afterward, eat it at least five days a week. Vary what you add to it so it stays interesting. On the other two days, eat a sandwich or soup with oil-free hummus (see page 112) and raw or steamed vegetables. Drink water with this meal.

FIGURE 1
Designing the quarter plate

Dinner: AROUND 5:00 P.M.

Dinner should be light. Imagine your dinner plate divided into quarters (see Figure 1). Half the plate should be filled with steamed or grilled vegetables to give yourself a break from the raw vegetables you ate at lunch. One-quarter of the plate should be the main course, such as brown rice and beans, quinoa and lentils, grilled tempeh burgers, or Black Bean and Corn Burritos (see page 64) made with whole-grain tortillas. The final quarter of the plate could be boiled or roasted potatoes. Drink water with this meal (add fruits to the water to flavor it, if desired).

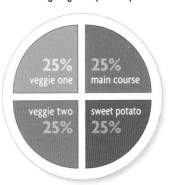

Dessert (optional) and Beyond

Dessert, if desired, should immediately follow dinner. It could be fruit or dark chocolate (at least 70 percent cacao) with unsweetened, no-salt-added peanut butter. Ideally, eat nothing after 6:00 p.m.

Do the best you can with your schedule. But remember, you don't need to eat much during the part of the day when you aren't particularly active.

To lose weight after the six week period, you can increase your fasting time if you have the approval of your physician.

THE MANY JOYS OF COOKING

There are so many benefits to cooking at home. With home cooking, you know where your food comes from, and you can turn that food into something your palate will savor and your body will appreciate. Preparing your own food helps to create a positive mind-body connection, and it's a wonderful way to express love for yourself as well as love for your family and friends. When you cook at home, you can be as creative and adventurous as you like. You can also make the experience a time of mindfulness as you see, smell, and touch the ingredients and turn them into powerfully healthy, aromatic dishes.

Please know that eating healthy does not have to be expensive. To save money, use dried beans rather than pricier canned beans. Buy fresh vegetables from local farmers markets or buy frozen veggies; both organic and nonorganic are fine. The goal is just to do your best. A bowl of brown rice and black beans with steamed fresh or frozen spinach can cost less than a dollar. Cooked rolled oats with fresh or frozen blueberries for breakfast is also a bargain. Sweet potatoes are filling and highly nutritious and can be served at any meal. Uncooked, they can be stored for a long time. Although hummus is readily available in stores, it's easy to make it at home, and it will cost a whole lot less. It certainly is possible to eat healthy on a budget. It may take a little more planning, but it absolutely can be done.

Preparing home-cooked meals can lead to a new world of healthy eating. This cookbook was developed for just that purpose. The recipes are simple and easy to follow and will enhance your enjoyment of both cooking and eating.

Cooking can be a joyful process, whether you prepare a meal for yourself, your family, or your community. It offers a welcome way to connect with others during times of stress, isolation, or celebration. As you follow a diverse plant-based diet, be aware that you are not only eating nutrient-rich food but also actively lowering inflammation and oxidative stress in your body, improving your gut-brain axis, and adding years to your life!

Summary

ood is part of living. What you eat should make you feel good. If food is making you feel bad, it may be time to make changes to your lifestyle and eating habits.

Below is a summary of what to eat and what to avoid, followed by a grocery list for getting started the first week. One serving equals one cup of uncooked vegetables, one-half cup of cooked vegetables, or a baseball-sized fruit.

WHAT TO INCLUDE

- Green leafy vegetables *(2–3 servings per day)*, the darker the better *(arugula, chard, escarole, kale, and spinach)*
- Other vegetables *(1–2 servings per day)*, such as beets, broccoli, cucumbers, and peppers *(orange, red, or yellow)*
- Berries, such as blackberries, blueberries, and strawberries, or any other fresh fruit that's low in sugar
- Whole grains, such as farro, millet, oats, quinoa, spelt, and whole wheat berries
- Legumes, including beans *(such as chickpeas)*, lentils, and split peas
- Nuts and seeds, such as almonds, chia seeds, flaxseeds, and walnuts
- Spices, such as basil, coriander, cumin, ginger, oregano, and turmeric
- Plant-derived protein, such as almonds, beans, chia seeds, lentils, quinoa, soybeans, split peas, tofu, and tempeh
- Water

WHAT TO AVOID

- Animal products (*dairy products, eggs, fish, meat, and poultry*)
- Processed and "instant" foods
- Foods with added sugar
- Fried foods

SUGGESTED GROCERY LIST FOR THE FIRST SIX WEEKS

- Avocados
- Balsamic vinegar
- Beans, dried or canned
- Black pepper, ground
- Blueberries and other berries and fruit
- Brown rice
- Chia seeds and/or flaxseeds
- Cinnamon, ground
- Ezekiel sprouted-grain bread or whole wheat bread without preservatives from your local bakery
- Hummus, oil-free
- Kale, especially baby kale, and other dark-green leafy vegetables (*arugula, escarole, spinach*)
- Kimchi or sauerkraut
- Lentils, cooked or canned
- Nut milk (*almond or another nondairy milk of your choice*), unsweetened
- Nutritional yeast flakes
- Nuts, oil-free, unsalted
- Oats, whole rolled or steel cut
- Roasted peanut butter or raw nut butter (*unsweetened, with no salt or oil added*)
- Quinoa
- Sweet potatoes
- Tempeh
- Tofu (*whole blocks*)
- Turmeric, ground
- Vegetables for salads (*choose a colorful variety*)
- Vitamin B_{12} supplement
- Vitamin D supplement (*if you have dark skin or are not spending time in the sun*)

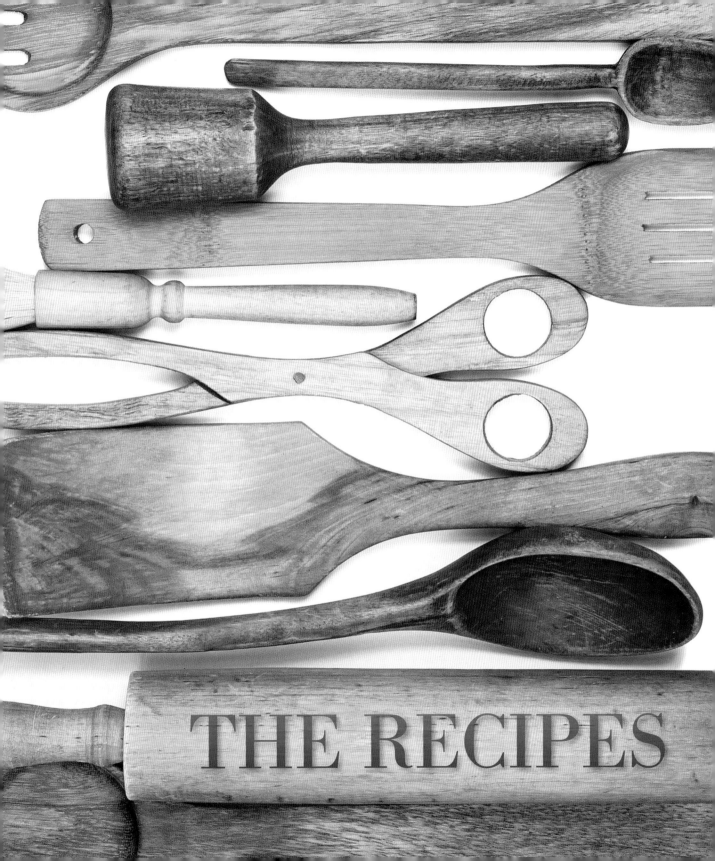

THE RECIPES

Morning Delights

Muesli

The combination of oats, nuts, and seeds alone is an energy powerhouse, but with the addition of nutrient-dense berries and apples, it's an unbeatable breakfast that will keep your blood sugar stable for hours. It's also a morning time-saver, since most of the prep is done the night before.

¾ cup whole **rolled oats**

¼ cup sliced **almonds**

¼ cup raw **sunflower seeds**

¼ cup raw **pumpkin seeds**

2 tablespoons shredded **dried coconut** (optional)

1 cup unsweetened **almond milk**

1 **apple**, peeled and diced

½ cup **raspberries**, **blueberries**, or sliced **strawberries**

Put the oats, almonds, sunflower seeds, pumpkin seeds, and optional coconut in a medium bowl. Add the almond milk and stir until well combined. Cover and refrigerate for 8 to 12 hours. Just before serving, add the apple and raspberries, and stir until evenly distributed. Serve immediately.

> **VARIATION:** Rather than dicing the apple, grate it directly into the bowl before adding the raspberries.

Mango-Turmeric Smoothie

This naturally sweet smoothie gets an anti-inflammatory boost from mango, dates, and turmeric.

1 cup unsweetened **almond milk**, plus more as needed

½ **fresh mango**, cut into chunks, or 1 cup **frozen mango** chunks

2 pitted medjool **dates** (optional)

2 teaspoons freshly squeezed **lime juice**

½ teaspoon **ground turmeric**

⅛ teaspoon **ground cardamom** (optional)

Put all the ingredients in a high-speed blender and process until smooth. If the mixture seems too thick, add a little more almond milk and process again. Serve immediately.

Mint-Flecked Smoothie

This smoothie is a wonderful morning eye-opener. Mint not only is refreshing but it also aids digestion.

1½ cups unsweetened **almond milk**

1 fresh or frozen **banana**, broken into chunks

½ cup **hemp seeds** (optional)

2 pitted medjool **dates**

¼ cup **fresh mint leaves**, firmly packed, or 4 teaspoons **dried mint**

Put all the ingredients in a high-speed blender and process until smooth. Serve immediately.

Orange-Ginger-Turmeric Smoothie

This smoothie makes an excellent light breakfast. In addition to anti-inflammatory ginger and turmeric, it's loaded with flavor and essential nutrients, including protein, vitamin C, and potassium.

2 **oranges**

1 cup unsweetened **almond milk**, plus more as needed

1 fresh or frozen **banana**, broken into chunks

½ cup **hemp seeds**

2 pitted medjool **dates** (optional)

1 tablespoon chopped **fresh ginger**, or ¼ teaspoon **ground ginger**

½ teaspoon **ground turmeric**

Finely grate the zest from the oranges (see tip) directly into a high-speed blender. Squeeze the juice from the oranges into a small bowl, remove any seeds, and pour the juice into the blender. Add the almond milk, banana, hemp seeds, dates, ginger, and turmeric. Process until smooth. If the mixture seems too thick, add a little more almond milk and process again. Serve immediately.

> TIP Use the fine side of a box grater or a vegetable peeler to carefully remove just the flavorful orange layer of zest.

Mango-Banana Smoothie

Creamy, with just a hint of green from the baby spinach, this smoothie gets its sweetness from ripe banana and mango. Beginning the day with dark leafy greens will give you a head start.

- 1 cup frozen **mango** chunks
- 1 frozen ripe **banana**
- ½ cup freshly squeezed **orange juice**
- ½ cup unsweetened **almond milk**
- ½ cup **baby spinach**, lightly packed

Put all the ingredients in a high-speed blender and process until smooth. Serve immediately.

Green Breakfast Smoothie

A terrific way to start the day, this smoothie is light, nutritious, and surprisingly filling. If your mornings are typically rushed, you can prep the kale the night before and simply transfer it to a blender in the morning.

1½ cups **water**

1 cup stemmed and coarsely chopped **kale leaves**, firmly packed

1 fresh or frozen **banana**, broken into chunks

2 **kiwis**, peeled, or 1 cup fresh or frozen **blueberries** or **mango** chunks

¼ cup **fresh mint leaves**, firmly packed, or 1 tablespoon **dried mint**

2 pitted medjool **dates** (optional)

1 tablespoon freshly squeezed **lime juice**

Put all the ingredients in a high-speed blender and process until smooth. Serve immediately.

VARIATION: Replace the kiwi with 1 Granny Smith or other tart green apple, peeled, cored, and cut into chunks.

TIP Either curly or Tuscan kale (also known as lacinato, Italian, dinosaur, or dino kale) will work in this recipe.

Avocado Toast

Few things rival a simple avocado toast for a quick snack or a side to accompany soup.

2 slices **whole-grain bread**, toasted

1 **avocado**, sliced

¼ **red onion**, thinly sliced or diced

1 **serrano chile**, finely diced

Sea salt

1 tablespoon coarsely chopped **fresh cilantro**

Top each piece of toast with half of the avocado slices, pressing the avocado down gently. Layer the onion and chile equally over the avocado and sprinkle lightly with salt. Sprinkle the cilantro equally over the top of each serving. Carefully cut each toast in half diagonally and serve immediately.

Tofu Scramble

Scrambled tofu is always a popular breakfast (or even lunch or dinner) choice because it's quick, easy, flavorful, and versatile, plus it's jam-packed with plant-based protein.

1 pound **firm tofu**

4 **scallions**, thinly sliced

½ teaspoon **ground turmeric**

¼ teaspoon **cayenne** (optional)

Sea salt

Freshly ground **black pepper**

Put the tofu in a medium bowl and crush and crumble it into small pieces using your hands.

Mist a skillet with olive oil spray and place over medium-high heat. Put the tofu, scallions, turmeric, and optional cayenne in the hot skillet and cook, stirring constantly, until the tofu is lightly browned and evenly stained yellow with the turmeric. Season to taste with salt and pepper.

VARIATION: Replace the scallions with diced red onion, diced red bell pepper, and/or chopped fresh basil, cilantro, parsley, or other fresh or dried herbs (such as basil, oregano, or tarragon) of your choice.

Chia Seed Pudding WITH KIWIS AND POMEGRANATES

MAKES 2 SERVINGS

Despite their small size, chia seeds are a potent combination of protein, omega-3 fatty acids, minerals, antioxidants, and soluble fiber, yet they are very low in calories. The combination of soaked chia seeds, kiwifruit, and pomegranate arils makes an energizing morning meal that will keep you satisfied until lunchtime.

2 cups unsweetened **almond milk**

¼ cup **chia seeds**

1 teaspoon **vanilla extract**

2 **kiwis**, peeled and diced

½ cup **pomegranate arils**

¼ teaspoon **ground cardamom** (optional)

Put the almond milk in a medium bowl. Add the chia seeds and vanilla and stir briskly for at least 1 minute to prevent the chia from clumping. Cover and let rest in the refrigerator for at least 20 minutes (see tip).

Just before serving, stir the chia mixture again. Add the kiwis, pomegranate arils, and optional cardamom. Divide between two small bowls and serve.

> TIP The almond milk and chia seed mixture can be made and stored in the refrigerator the night before. In the morning, you will only need to prepare and add the fruit and optional cardamom.

Oatmeal Breakfast Muffins

Like all muffins, these are best right out of the oven.

1 tablespoon ground brown or golden **flaxseeds**

3 tablespoons **water**

1½ cups **whole wheat flour**

¾ cup whole **rolled oats**

⅓ cup **walnuts**, coarsely chopped

2 teaspoons **baking powder**

½ teaspoon **sea salt**

1 cup unsweetened **almond milk**

3 tablespoons extra-virgin **olive oil**

2 tablespoons **Date Paste** (page 127)

½ cup unsweetened **dried blueberries**

Preheat the oven to 400 degrees F. Mist a 12-cup muffin tin with olive oil spray.

Put the flaxseeds in a small bowl. Add the water and stir well. Let rest for 15 minutes.

Put the flour, oats, walnuts, baking powder, and salt in a large bowl. Stir until well combined.

Put the almond milk, flaxseed mixture, oil, and Date Paste in a medium bowl. Pour into the dry ingredients and add the blueberries. Stir briefly, just until combined. Spoon into the prepared muffin cups. Bake for 20 minutes, until a toothpick inserted in the middle of a muffin comes out clean.

TIP Tightly wrap any leftover muffins in plastic wrap as soon as they have cooled. Serve them the following day or store in the freezer for up to three months.

Tropical Quinoa Cereal

Quinoa is easy to digest and high in protein. It provides all nine essential amino acids as well as minerals, fiber, and antioxidants, making it an outstanding breakfast choice.

3 cups unsweetened **apple juice**

¼ teaspoon **sea salt**

1 cup **quinoa**

⅓ cup diced unsweetened **dried papaya**

⅓ cup diced unsweetened **dried mango**

⅓ cup diced **fresh pineapple**

½ teaspoon **ground cinnamon**

½ teaspoon **ground cardamom**

Pinch **ground cloves** (optional)

Pinch **ground allspice** (optional)

1 **banana**, cut into ½-inch pieces

Put the juice and salt in a medium saucepan over medium-high heat and bring to a boil. Add the quinoa, papaya, mango, pineapple, cinnamon, cardamom, optional cloves, and optional allspice and stir to combine. As soon as the mixture returns to a boil, decrease the heat to medium, cover the saucepan, and cook for 20 minutes. Remove from the heat and stir in the banana. Serve immediately.

> TIP If you prefer fresh papaya and mango, use ½ cup of the diced fresh fruit in place of the dried fruit and add it along with the banana.

Buckwheat WITH APPLE AND DRIED APRICOTS

Hearty and warming, buckwheat makes an excellent breakfast food. Surprisingly, buckwheat is a seed, not a grain, and it is higher in protein and lower in carbohydrates than most grains. It will digest slowly and evenly and sustain you for hours.

3 cups **water**

⅓ cup brown **buckwheat**

1 teaspoon **sea salt**

½ teaspoon extra-virgin **olive oil**

1 **apple**, peeled and cut into bite-size pieces

¼ teaspoon **ground cinnamon**

1 cup unsweetened **almond milk**

⅓ cup **dried apricots**, diced

½ teaspoon **vanilla extract**

Put the water in a medium saucepan over high heat and bring to a boil. Add the buckwheat and salt. Cook, stirring occasionally, for 7 minutes, then drain in a strainer.

Put the oil in a medium saucepan over medium-high heat. Add the apple and cook, stirring constantly, until the apple is very lightly browned, about 4 minutes. Add the cinnamon and stir briefly. Add the buckwheat, almond milk, apricots, and vanilla extract. Bring to a boil, then decrease the heat to medium. Cook, stirring occasionally, until thickened, about 5 minutes.

Whole Wheat Pancakes WITH MIXED BERRY SAUCE

Berries make a delicious, naturally sweet topping for these light and fluffy pancakes.

2 tablespoons **ground flaxseeds**

6 tablespoons **water**

2 cups frozen mixed **berries**, thawed

3 tablespoons **Date Paste** (page 127)

1 teaspoon **vanilla extract**

1 teaspoon **almond extract**

Pinch ground **cinnamon**

1½ cups **whole wheat flour**

1 tablespoon **baking powder**

½ teaspoon **sea salt**

¾ cup unsweetened **almond milk**, plus more as needed

1 tablespoon extra-virgin **olive oil**

Put the flaxseeds in a small bowl. Add the water and stir to combine. Let rest for 15 minutes.

Put the berries, 2 tablespoons of the Date Paste, and the vanilla extract, almond extract, and cinnamon in a medium bowl. Stir and gently mash the berries to release some of their juices. Set aside.

Put the flour, baking powder, and salt in a medium bowl. Stir with a dry whisk to combine. Make a well in the center.

Put the almond milk, remaining tablespoon of Date Paste, and the oil in a small bowl. Add the flaxseed mixture and whisk until well combined. Pour into the center of the flour mixture and whisk using a circular motion, starting from the center, until all the flour has been incorporated. If the mixture is very thick, add more almond milk, 1 tablespoon at a time, to create a thick but pourable batter.

Mist a skillet with olive oil spray and place over medium-high heat until hot. Scoop out ¼ cup of the batter and pour it into the skillet. Spread the batter into a three-inch circle with the back of a spoon. Cook until bubbles form on the surface and the underside is lightly browned, about 2 minutes. Flip the pancake and cook the other side until the pancake feels spongy when lightly pressed, about 1 minute. Repeat with the remaining batter. Serve the pancakes immediately with the reserved berry sauce.

CHAPTER

9

Soups and Sandwiches

Miso Soup WITH CHARD AND TOFU

MAKES 4 SERVINGS

Miso soup is warming, alkalizing, and highly nutritious. As miso contains vital probiotics, stir it in only after the soup has been removed from the heat in order to preserve its beneficial properties. Miso can be found in the refrigerated section of natural food stores.

8 cups (2 quarts) unsalted **vegetable broth**

½ cup mellow **white miso**

2 tablespoons hot (not boiling) **water**

1 cup stemmed and very thinly sliced or finely chopped **green Swiss chard** or coarsely chopped **baby spinach**, firmly packed

8 ounces **firm tofu**, finely diced

1 cup thinly sliced **scallions**

Put the broth in a large saucepan and bring to a simmer over medium heat.

Put the miso in a small bowl. Add the water and whisk until smooth. Set aside.

Add the chard, tofu, and scallions to the simmering broth and cook, stirring occasionally, for 5 minutes. Remove from the heat and stir in the miso mixture until well combined. Serve immediately.

Asparagus and Parsley Soup

MAKES 4 SERVINGS

This soup is a gorgeous green, the very essence of spring, and it's about as simple as soup can get. Be sure to use the most tender young asparagus you can find, the thinner the better. Asparagus are valuable prebiotics and fresh parsley is an excellent source of antioxidants that soothe inflammation.

2¼ pounds thin, young **asparagus**

½ cup minced **shallots** or **onion**

4 cups unsalted **vegetable broth** or **water**

¼ teaspoon **sea salt**

½ cup plus 1 tablespoon stemmed and coarsely chopped **flat-leaf parsley**, firmly packed

Freshly ground **black pepper**

Wash the asparagus and pat dry. Snap off the tough bottom portion of each spear and discard. Cut off the tips uniformly, 1½ inches long, and set aside. Slice the stalks into ¼-inch pieces.

Mist a large saucepan with olive oil spray and place over medium-high heat. When hot, add the shallots. Decrease the heat to medium and cook, stirring constantly, until the shallots just begin to sizzle, about 1 minute. Decrease the heat to low and spread out the shallots in an even layer. Cover and cook for 15 minutes, stirring occasionally. Add a tablespoon of water, if needed, to prevent sticking.

Uncover and add the broth and salt. Increase the heat to high and bring to a boil. Add the sliced asparagus stems. Adjust the heat to maintain a simmer and cook until the asparagus is very tender, about 15 minutes.

Fill a medium saucepan with water and bring to a boil over medium-high heat. Add the asparagus tips and cook, stirring occasionally, until just tender but still firm, about 2 minutes. Drain, refresh under cold water, and drain thoroughly. Reserve 8 of the best-looking tips and put the rest in a high-speed blender.

When the asparagus stems are finished cooking, add them to the blender along with the broth and ½ cup of the parsley (reserve the remaining tablespoon of parsley for garnish). Process until smooth and bright green. Reheat if needed.

Ladle the soup into four bowls. Place two of the reserved asparagus tips in the middle of each bowl, forming an X. Sprinkle with the reserved tablespoon of parsley. Serve immediately.

Carrot Soup WITH GINGER AND TURMERIC

This carrot soup is a high-powered, anti-inflammatory flavor fest. Be sure to include the black pepper, as it contains a compound called piperine that dramatically increases the body's absorption of the anti-inflammatory phytonutrient curcumin from the turmeric.

½ teaspoon **cumin seeds**

½ teaspoon **black mustard seeds**

1 **onion**, diced

4 cloves **garlic**, minced

4 cups grated **carrots**

½ teaspoon **sea salt**

1 cup unsalted **vegetable broth**

1 cup unsweetened **almond milk**

1 tablespoon coarsely chopped **fresh ginger**, or 1 teaspoon **ground ginger**

1 teaspoon **ground turmeric**

¼ teaspoon **ground cardamom**

¼ teaspoon **ground cinnamon**

Freshly ground **black pepper**

2 tablespoons coarsely chopped **fresh cilantro** or **parsley**, for garnish

Mist a large saucepan with olive oil spray and place over medium-high heat. When hot, add the cumin seeds and mustard seeds and cook, stirring once or twice, until the seeds begin to pop and release their aroma, 1 to 2 minutes. Decrease the heat to medium, add the onion and cook, stirring frequently, until the onion begins to soften, about 5 minutes. Add the garlic and cook, stirring constantly, for 1 minute. Add a tablespoon of water, if needed, to prevent sticking. Add the carrots and salt and cook, stirring constantly, until almost dry, about 4 minutes. Add the vegetable broth and stir well. Increase the heat to high and bring to a boil. Adjust the heat to maintain a simmer and cook, stirring occasionally, until the vegetables are very tender, about 20 minutes.

Transfer the soup to a high-speed blender. Add the almond milk, ginger, turmeric, cardamom, and cinnamon and process until smooth. Pour back into the saucepan. Season with pepper to taste and reheat until hot. Ladle into bowls and garnish with the cilantro. Serve immediately.

Minestrone Verde

This thick, hearty vegetable soup is fortified with beans and potatoes and makes for a full meal. It's loaded with dark leafy greens and is enhanced with a lively pesto.

1 stalk **celery**, diced

1 **onion**, diced

4 cloves **garlic**, minced

4 cups unsalted **vegetable broth**

1 bunch **curly** or **Tuscan kale**, stemmed and chopped

1 bunch **red** or **rainbow Swiss chard**, leaves chopped and stems sliced

2 **zucchini**, diced

1 large **russet potato**, with skin, diced

1 cup fresh or frozen **green beans**, cut in ½-inch lengths

½ cup frozen **green peas**

½ teaspoon **sea salt**

1 (15-ounce) **can no-salt-added cannellini beans**, rinsed and drained

1 cup **Basil Pesto** (page 120)

Mist a large saucepan with olive oil spray and place over medium heat. When hot, add the celery, onion, and garlic and stir well. Shake the saucepan to spread the vegetables into an even layer, cover, and decrease the heat to low. Let the vegetables sweat for 15 minutes, stirring occasionally. Add 1 tablespoon of water, if needed, to prevent sticking.

Add the vegetable broth, increase the heat to high, and bring to a boil. Add the kale, chard, zucchini, potato, green beans, peas, and salt. Return to a boil, then immediately adjust the heat to maintain a bare simmer, and cook, uncovered, for 2 hours.

Add the cannellini beans and warm through. Remove from the heat and stir in the pesto. Serve immediately.

Chilled Avocado Soup

This cold soup with a hint of heat is ideal to serve during hot weather.

2 white onions, minced

3 stalks **celery**, strings removed and minced

2 **serrano chiles**, seeded and minced

3 cloves of **garlic**, minced

1 (1-inch) piece **fresh ginger**, peeled and minced, or 1 teaspoon **ground ginger**

1 teaspoon **ground coriander**

½ teaspoon **sea salt**

4 cups unsalted **vegetable broth**

2 teaspoons **dried tarragon**

3 large ripe **avocados**

1 tablespoon freshly squeezed **lime juice**

1 tablespoon minced **fresh parsley**, for garnish

Mist a large, heavy saucepan with olive oil spray and place over low heat. Add the onion, celery, chiles, garlic, ginger, coriander, and salt and stir well. Cover and let the vegetables sweat, stirring occasionally, for 10 minutes. Add tablespoons of water, as needed, to keep the mixture moist.

Add the broth and tarragon. Increase the heat to medium and simmer for 10 minutes. Remove from the heat and let cool.

While the soup is cooking, cut the avocado into chunks and put in a medium bowl. Add the lime juice and toss until evenly distributed. Transfer the avocados to a blender, add the cooled soup, and process until smooth. Strain through a fine-mesh strainer. Cover and refrigerate until cold, at least 3 hours.

Just before serving, whisk thoroughly. Ladle into chilled bowls and garnish with the parsley.

Soothing Kale Soup

MAKES 4 SERVINGS

This creamy, dairy-free soup calls for minimal ingredients, which allows the kale to take center stage. Once the ingredients are prepped, it can be cooked and on the table in under twenty minutes.

1 **onion**, diced

2 **russet** or 4 **Yukon Gold potatoes**, peeled and cubed

2 cloves **garlic**, minced

3¼ cups unsalted **vegetable broth**

2 cups **curly** or **Tuscan kale**, chopped

1 cup unsweetened **almond milk** or **soymilk**

Cayenne

Smoked paprika

Sea salt

Freshly ground **black pepper**

¼ cup raw **pumpkin seeds**, for garnish

¼ cup raw **sunflower seeds**, for garnish

Mist a large saucepan with olive oil spray and place over medium-high heat. Add the onion, potatoes, and garlic and cook, stirring almost constantly, for 5 minutes. Add water, 1 tablespoon at a time, if needed to prevent sticking. Add the broth and bring to a simmer. Add the kale and cook, stirring occasionally, until the kale and potatoes are tender, about 10 minutes.

Carefully transfer the soup to a high-speed blender and process until smooth. Return the soup to the saucepan and stir in the almond milk. Season with cayenne, smoked paprika, salt, and pepper to taste and reheat over medium-low. Serve hot, garnished with the pumpkin and sunflower seeds.

Curried Pumpkin Soup WITH PUMPKIN SEEDS

A high-quality curry powder can elevate the flavor of a dish from pedestrian to sublime, and, as a bonus, virtually all the spices in curry powder are anti-inflammatory.

1 large **onion**, diced

8 cloves **garlic**, minced

3 tablespoons peeled and finely diced **fresh ginger**, or 1 tablespoon **ground ginger**

1 tablespoon **curry powder**

¾ teaspoon **sea salt**

4½ cups peeled and diced **pumpkin** or **butternut squash** (about 2 pounds)

5 cups unsalted **vegetable broth**

1 can (14 ounces) light **coconut milk**

¼ cup raw **pumpkin seeds**, for garnish

Fresh cilantro leaves, for garnish

Mist a large saucepan with olive oil spray and place over medium-high heat. When hot, decrease the heat to medium, add the onion, and cook, stirring constantly, until the onion softens, 2 to 3 minutes. Add the garlic and ginger and continue to cook, stirring constantly, for 2 minutes. Add the curry powder and salt and stir to combine. Add the pumpkin and cook, stirring constantly, until the mixture is nearly dry.

Add the vegetable broth and coconut milk. Increase the heat to high and bring to a boil. Adjust the heat to maintain a steady simmer and cook until the vegetables are very tender, about 20 minutes.

Transfer the soup to a high-speed blender and process until smooth. Pour back into the saucepan and reheat.

Ladle into bowls. Garnish with the pumpkin seeds and cilantro leaves, and serve immediately.

Black Bean Soup WITH A SECRET

MAKES 4 SERVINGS

Although there's just a hint of cocoa in this soup, it lends an elegant flavor and aroma. Pure cocoa with nothing added is a miraculous food, replete with antioxidants and minerals, especially magnesium. It's also very rich in flavonoids. The botanical name for cocoa, Theobroma, *means "food of the gods" in Greek, which pretty much says it all.*

1 **red onion**, diced

3 **bay leaves**

½ teaspoon **sea salt**

2 stalks **celery**, diced

2 **carrots**, diced

1 **red bell pepper**, seeded and diced

1 cup no-salt-added **tomato purée**

4 cups unsalted **vegetable broth**

2 (15-ounce) cans no-salt-added **black beans**, undrained

1 tablespoon unsweetened **Dutch-processed cocoa**

½ teaspoon freshly ground **black pepper**

½ teaspoon **smoked paprika**

½ cup coarsely chopped **fresh cilantro** or **parsley**, packed

Mist a large saucepan with olive oil spray and place over medium-high heat. When hot, decrease the heat to medium and add the onion, bay leaves, and salt. Cook, stirring constantly, until the onion softens, about 5 minutes. Add the celery, carrots, and bell pepper and cook, stirring constantly, until all the vegetables are softened, about 10 minutes. Add water, 1 tablespoon at a time, as needed to prevent sticking. Add the tomato purée and broth and bring to a boil. Adjust the heat to maintain a simmer and cook until the vegetables are very tender, about 15 minutes.

Stir in the beans and their liquid, cocoa, pepper, and smoked paprika. Return to a simmer and cook for 5 minutes, stirring occasionally. Remove from the heat and stir in the cilantro. Serve immediately.

Seitan Tacos WITH GREEN SAUCE

White corn tortillas are made with white corn, which is a whole grain, just like its yellow counterpart. White corn, however, is generally softer and more tender, so tortillas made from it are better suited for tacos, like these, that are rolled. Be forewarned that eating these tacos can be a bit messy, but that's just part of the fun.

1 bunch **cilantro**, coarsely chopped, stems included (about 1 cup)

1 (16-ounce) jar **salsa verde** (Mexican green sauce)

4 cloves **garlic**, minced or pressed

1 or 2 **serrano chiles** (optional)

1 pound plain **seitan**, cut into ½-inch-thick strips

12 **white corn tortillas**

1 small **red onion**, finely diced

Cashew Crema (page 127)

Set aside one-quarter of the chopped cilantro and cover it with plastic wrap. Put the remaining chopped cilantro and the salsa verde, garlic, and optional chiles in a blender and process until smooth. Transfer to a medium saucepan and place over medium-low heat.

Put a large skillet over a high heat until hot. Mist the skillet with olive oil spray and immediately add the seitan. Cook, stirring occasionally, until lightly browned. Transfer to the saucepan with the green sauce.

Heat the tortillas, one at a time, over an open flame or on a hot skillet until lightly charred. As they come off the heat, store them, stacked, in a folded towel to keep warm.

Put the seitan and sauce in a bowl and serve with the tortillas, onion, and Cashew Crema.

To make the tacos, put a warm tortilla in one hand and scoop a small portion of the seitan and sauce in the center. Add a little of the onion and a drizzle of the crema, then roll up the tortilla, enclosing the filling. Hold the taco over a plate as you eat in order to catch the sauce and bits that will inevitably drip out.

Black Bean and Corn Burritos

Two flavorful fillings are stuffed into multigrain tortillas to create a nutrient-packed, fiber-rich, satisfying lunch, dinner, or even breakfast.

1 medium **red onion**, finely diced

4 cloves **garlic**, minced or pressed

1 (15-ounce) can no-salt-added **black beans**, rinsed and drained

2 teaspoons freshly squeezed **lime juice**

¼ cup coarsely chopped **cilantro**, packed

Sea salt

½ **roasted red pepper**, finely diced

1½ cups **frozen corn** kernels, thawed, or **canned corn**, drained

½ teaspoon **smoked paprika**

4 **multigrain tortillas**

Mist a medium saucepan with olive oil spray and place over medium-high heat for 30 seconds. Add the onion and garlic and cook, stirring frequently, until the onions are soft, about 4 minutes. Scoop out about half the mixture and set aside. Add the beans. Cook, lightly mashing the beans to create a thick, chunky consistency. Remove from the heat and stir in the lime juice and cilantro. Season with salt to taste. Cover to keep warm.

Put the reserved onion and garlic, roasted red pepper, and corn in a small saucepan over medium heat. Cook, stirring constantly, until hot. Add the smoked paprika and season with salt to taste. Remove from the heat and cover to keep warm.

Put a skillet over medium heat. Put a tortilla in the pan and heat it lightly, turning it once or twice, just until warm and softened. Transfer the tortilla to a large plate. Spoon one-quarter of the bean mixture and one-quarter of the corn mixture side by side in the center of the tortilla. Fold one side of the tortilla over, just covering the beans and vegetables. Fold the two adjacent sides over, pressing gently to enclose the filling. Roll the package over the remaining side of the tortilla to form the burrito. Cover to keep warm. Repeat with the remaining tortillas and fillings.

Chickpea Salad Sandwiches

This wholesome salad makes a nourishing sandwich filling on its own or with lettuce leaves and tomato slices. You could also wrap it in a whole-grain tortilla, stuff it into whole wheat pita pockets, or mound it on a bed of lettuce or spinach. Dill pickles on the side are always a welcome touch.

1 (15-ounce) can **chickpeas**, drained and rinsed

½ cup diced **celery**

½ cup diced **red** or **yellow bell pepper** or shredded **carrot**

2 tablespoons **Dijon** or **yellow mustard**

2 tablespoons **tahini**

2 tablespoons unsweetened **dried cranberries** or **raisins**

2 teaspoons **dried dill weed**

1 teaspoon **garlic powder**

¼ teaspoon **sea salt**, plus more as needed

¼ teaspoon freshly ground **black pepper**, plus more as needed

Put the chickpeas in a medium bowl and coarsely mash using a fork or potato masher. For better texture, don't overmash and try to keep a few of the chickpeas whole. Add the celery, bell pepper, mustard, tahini, cranberries, dill weed, garlic powder, salt, and pepper and stir until well combined. Taste and add more salt or pepper if desired. Stored in a sealed container in the refrigerator, the salad will keep for up to four days.

Hot Tempeh Sandwiches WITH COLESLAW

Whoever wrote "Simplicity is the ultimate sophistication," must have been dreaming of these sandwiches.

8 ounces **tempeh**, cut horizontally into two rectangular slices

2 **whole-grain sandwich rolls**, lightly toasted

2 cups **Coleslaw with Savory Peanut Dressing** (page 97)

Mist the tempeh slices on both sides with olive oil spray. Place a skillet over high heat until hot. Mist with olive oil spray and add the tempeh slices. Cook until lightly browned, about 3 minutes per side.

Put the coleslaw in a strainer set over a bowl and press down gently to drain any excess liquid. Spread about ⅓ cup of the coleslaw on the bottom half of each roll. Place the hot tempeh slices over the slaw and divide the remaining slaw between the sandwiches, spreading it over the tempeh. Cover with the roll tops, pressing down gently. Cut the sandwiches in half, if desired, and serve immediately.

Barbecued Tempeh Sandwiches

These mouthwatering, high-protein sandwiches come together lickety-split. If time is uber short, purchase pre-shredded cabbage from the grocery store.

¾ cup **Barbecue Sauce** (page 123)

1 (8-ounce) package **tempeh**

2 cups thinly sliced or shredded **napa cabbage** or other cabbage

2 whole-grain **sandwich rolls** or **buns**, sliced in half horizontally

Put the sauce in a small saucepan over medium-low heat.

Slice the tempeh in half horizontally. Cut each piece into 2 equal pieces. Put the tempeh in a steamer and steam for about 5 minutes. Immediately add it to the barbeque sauce. Gently toss to coat the tempeh evenly.

Heat a grill or grill pan until hot (see tip).

Remove the tempeh slices from the sauce, scraping any clinging sauce back into the saucepan. Mist the pieces lightly with olive oil spray and place them on the grill. Grill until nicely marked, about 2 minutes. Turn the slices over and brush lightly with the sauce. Cook until marked, 1 to 2 minutes.

Spread half the sauce on the rolls, coating bottoms and tops. Place two slices of the tempeh on each roll, overlapping them slightly. Spread the remaining sauce over the tempeh. Divide the cabbage between the sandwiches, piling it and then pressing it down gently. Cover with the tops of the rolls. Cut the sandwiches in half, if desired, and serve immediately.

> TIP If you don't have a grill or grill pan, you can broil the tempeh. Move the oven rack to the highest position and preheat the broiler for 5 to 10 minutes. Line a baking sheet with foil. Place the tempeh slices in a single layer on the prepared baking sheet, mist lightly with olive oil spray, and broil until browned. Turn the slices over and brown the other side, checking often to make sure the tempeh doesn't burn. Proceed with the recipe as directed.

Blazing Seitan Sandwiches

If you like hot seasonings, this sandwich filling of tender sliced seitan and massaged kale will have smoke coming out of your ears, yet you'll savor every bite.

1 bunch **Tuscan kale**, center ribs removed

1 teaspoon extra-virgin **olive oil**

⅛ teaspoon **sea salt**

1 large **onion**, thinly sliced

7 cloves **garlic**, minced or pressed

1 cup no-salt-added **tomato purée**

1 tablespoon **hot smoked paprika** or **smoked paprika**

2 teaspoons **cayenne**

8 ounces **seitan**, thinly sliced

2 **sandwich rolls**, cut in half lengthwise

Stack the kale leaves on a cutting board and thinly slice crosswise into strips. Transfer the kale to a large bowl. Put 1 teaspoon extra-virgin olive oil and ⅛ teaspoon sea salt in the palm of one hand. Put your palms together and rub briefly to spread the oil and salt to both hands. Massage the kale firmly with your hands until it becomes soft and silky, about 3 minutes.

Place a medium saucepan over medium-high heat until hot. Mist with olive oil spray and add the onion. Cook, stirring often, until the onion slices soften and begin to brown, about 7 minutes. Add the garlic and cook, stirring frequently, for 3 minutes. Add the tomato purée, smoked paprika, and cayenne. Cook, stirring constantly, until thoroughly combined, about 1 minute. Add the seitan and mix well. Cook, stirring frequently, until the sauce has thickened and the seitan is hot, about 5 minutes.

Toast the sandwich rolls, if desired. Divide the seitan between the bottom halves, spreading it out evenly. Divide the kale between the two sandwiches, spreading it over the seitan. Cover with the roll tops. Cut the sandwiches in half, if desired, and serve immediately.

Avocado and Chickpea Sandwiches

Now this is a sandwich you can really sink your teeth into! It makes a substantial lunch or dinner and is fast and fun to prepare.

1 cup cooked or canned **chickpeas**, rinsed and drained

1 tablespoon freshly squeezed **lemon juice**

2 cloves **garlic**, minced or pressed

1 teaspoon **smoked paprika**

2 **avocados**, peeled, pits removed

1 small **red onion**, finely diced

8 slices **whole-grain bread**

1 large **tomato**, thinly sliced

2 cups **baby arugula**

Put the chickpeas, lemon juice, garlic, and smoked paprika in a medium bowl. Mash the chickpeas lightly, just breaking them up and combining them well with the other ingredients. Dice the avocados and add them to the bowl along with the onion. Mash the mixture slightly, leaving some bits of avocado and chickpea for texture.

Toast the bread, if desired. Divide the avocado-chickpea mash among four of the slices, spreading it evenly. Divide the tomato slices among the sandwiches, arranging them on top of the mash. Cover with the arugula and place the remaining slices of bread on top. Cut the sandwiches in half, corner to corner, if desired.

10

Side Dishes

Sautéed Brussels Sprouts WITH GINGER

The secret to great Brussels sprouts is not overcooking them. By quartering them, the required cooking time to reach peak tenderness is decreased, ensuring that they aren't crunchy or mushy.

1½ tablespoons extra-virgin **olive oil**

1½ pounds **Brussels sprouts**, quartered lengthwise

1 (3-inch) piece **fresh ginger**, peeled, sliced crosswise, and cut into thin strips

2 teaspoons freshly squeezed **lime** or **lemon juice**

¼ teaspoon **cayenne**

Sea salt

Freshly ground **black pepper**

Put the oil in a large skillet over medium-high heat. When hot, add the Brussels sprouts and cook, stirring almost constantly, until lightly browned and tender-crisp. Add the ginger, lime juice, and cayenne and stir until evenly distributed. Season with salt and pepper to taste. Serve immediately.

Saag

For people who think they hate spinach, this recipe is the cure. Not only is this spinach dish good for you, it's just plain good!

1¼ pounds **spinach**

2 tablespoons extra-virgin **olive oil**

¼ teaspoon **cumin seeds**

7 **fenugreek seeds**

7 **fresh curry leaves** (optional)

1 cup finely diced **red onion**

2 teaspoons grated **fresh ginger**

3 cloves **garlic**, minced or pressed

½ teaspoon **ground turmeric**

½ teaspoon **ground coriander**

¼ teaspoon **cayenne**

½ teaspoon **sea salt**

Remove any coarse stems from the spinach. Fill a large saucepan with water and bring to a boil over high heat. Add the spinach and stir to submerge all the leaves. Drain in a colander. Shake to release water and lightly squeeze the spinach to extract most of the remaining water.

Heat the oil in a medium saucepan over medium-high heat. Add the cumin seeds and cook until the seeds release their aroma, 3 to 4 seconds. Add the fenugreek seeds and curry leaves and stir for 3 seconds. Add the onion, ginger, and garlic and stir briskly for 3 seconds. Decrease the heat to medium-low. Cook for 6 minutes, stirring frequently to prevent sticking. Add the turmeric, coriander, cayenne, and salt and stir until incorporated. Add the spinach and cook, stirring constantly, until wilted and well combined with the seasonings. Continue cooking until the spinach is tender, 8 to 10 minutes. Add water, 1 tablespoon at a time, if needed to prevent sticking.

 Fenugreek seeds and curry leaves are available at most spice shops, natural food stores, and Indian markets.

Mustard Greens WITH GOLDEN BEETS

MAKES 4 SERVINGS

Mustard greens are highly nutritious but a little on the bitter side. Cooking them with golden beets mellows that slight bitterness while boosting the nutritional value.

- 2 large **golden beets**, diced
- ¼ cup unsalted **vegetable broth**
- 2 large bunches (6 or 7 stems each) very fresh **mustard greens**, center ribs removed, leaves coarsely chopped
- 1 tablespoon low-sodium **soy sauce** or **liquid aminos**
- **Sriracha sauce** (optional)

Put the beets in a steamer and steam until just tender, about 15 minutes.

Put the vegetable broth and mustard greens in a large saucepan over medium-high heat. Cook, stirring constantly, until the greens wilt, about 2 minutes. Add the beets and soy sauce and cook, stirring almost constantly, until the mustard greens are just tender, about 2 minutes. Season with sriracha sauce to taste, if desired. Serve immediately.

Sautéed Kale WITH PINE NUT–RED PEPPER SAUCE

MAKES 4 SERVINGS

This very simple dish is very easy to prepare—the sauce can be made while the kale is cooking—but the flavor is complex.

- 1 tablespoon extra-virgin **olive oil**
- 1 **red onion**, diced
- 2 bunches **green kale**, stemmed and coarsely chopped
- 1 cup **Pine Nut–Red Pepper Sauce** (page 124)

Put the oil in a large saucepan over medium-high heat. When hot, add the onion and cook, stirring frequently, until the onion starts to brown, 5 to 7 minutes. Add the kale and cook, stirring frequently, until wilted and tender, 12 to 15 minutes. Add the sauce and cook, stirring constantly, until any excess liquid has been absorbed. Serve immediately.

Tuscan Kale WITH OLIVES, CAPERS, AND HAZELNUTS

Kale has enjoyed rockstar status in recent years, and for good reason. Not only is it loaded with beneficial nutrients, but it also can be prepared in countless ways.

1 cup **hazelnuts**

2 bunches **Tuscan kale**, stemmed and coarsely chopped

½ cup pitted **green olives**

1 tablespoon **capers**

Zest and juice of 1 **lemon**

¼ teaspoon **cayenne**

Sea salt

Freshly ground **black pepper**

Preheat the oven to 375 degrees F. Spread the hazelnuts on a baking sheet and roast until lightly browned, 7 to 10 minutes. Transfer nuts to a clean towel, wrap tightly, and let rest for 10 minutes. Roll the towel with the palm of one hand to loosen the skins. Unwrap and remove the nuts, dusting off any clinging bits of skin. Coarsely chop the nuts.

Fill a large saucepan with water and place over medium-high heat. When the water comes to a gentle boil, add the kale and cook, stirring occasionally, until just tender, 12 to 15 minutes. Drain in a colander and rinse with cold water. Squeeze the kale to remove as much water as possible. Return to the saucepan and place over medium heat. Cook, stirring occasionally, until the kale is hot.

Coarsely chop the olives and capers together, just until the pieces are about the same size as the chopped hazelnuts. Put in a medium bowl with the hazelnuts, lemon zest and juice, and cayenne and stir to combine. Add to the kale and stir until evenly distributed. Season with salt and pepper to taste. Serve immediately.

Tuscan Kale WITH ARUGULA AND HERBS

The combination of kale with arugula is a flavor triumph, but with the addition of shallots and herbs, it enters another galaxy.

4 cups **Tuscan kale**

2 teaspoons extra-virgin **olive oil**

2 **shallots**, minced

½ cup dry **white wine**

3 cups **baby arugula**

¼ cup chopped **fresh parsley**, lightly packed

2 tablespoons snipped **chives**

1 tablespoon chopped **fresh tarragon**, or 1 teaspoon **dried tarragon**

1 teaspoon coarsely chopped **fresh thyme**, or ¼ teaspoon **dried thyme**

Sea salt

Freshly ground **black pepper**

Remove the center ribs from the kale. Stack the kale leaves and cut into 1-inch pieces. Put the oil in a medium saucepan over medium heat. When hot, add the shallots and cook, stirring frequently, until soft, 4 to 5 minutes. Increase the heat to medium-high. When the shallots are just starting to brown, add the kale and cook, stirring constantly, until wilted. Add the wine and cook, stirring frequently, until the kale is tender, 10 to 15 minutes. If the mixture starts to dry out, add water, 1 tablespoon at a time, to prevent sticking or burning.

When the kale is tender, add the arugula, parsley, chives, tarragon, and thyme. Cook, stirring constantly, until fragrant, 2 to 3 minutes. Season with salt and pepper to taste. Serve immediately.

Creamed Swiss Chard

In the family of greens, Swiss chard is the middle child between kale and spinach. It's not as tender as spinach and not as tough as kale. This method of preparation will pleasantly surprise anyone who dislikes cooked greens.

8 cups stemmed **Swiss chard leaves**, packed

¼ teaspoon **sea salt**

2 teaspoons **cornstarch**

2 cups unsweetened **almond milk**

Ground nutmeg

Freshly ground **black pepper**

Fill a large saucepan with water and bring to a boil over high heat. Add the Swiss chard and cook for 1 minute. Drain in a colander and press down to express as much water as possible. Coarsely chop the chard and return it to the saucepan. Place over medium-high heat, add the salt, and stir to combine. Decrease the heat to medium.

Put the cornstarch in a medium bowl. Gradually whisk in the almond milk until smooth.

Pour into the saucepan, stir well, and cook, stirring frequently, until the almond milk has reduced and thickened. Season with nutmeg and pepper to taste. Serve immediately.

Roasted Asparagus WITH SESAME SAUCE

Roasting asparagus does amazing things for its flavor and texture.

¼ cup low-sodium **soy sauce**

2 tablespoons **rice vinegar**

3½ teaspoons **toasted sesame oil**

1½ pounds **asparagus**

1½ teaspoons extra-virgin **olive oil**

¼ teaspoon **sea salt**

2 tablespoons snipped **chives**

Preheat the oven to 475 degrees F. For the sesame sauce, put the soy sauce, vinegar, and 1½ teaspoons of the toasted sesame oil in a small bowl. Whisk until well combined and set aside.

Snap any tough, woody stems off the asparagus and discard. Rinse the asparagus and pat dry with a towel. Spread out the stalks on a baking sheet. Put the remaining 2 teaspoons of toasted sesame oil and the olive oil in a small cup and stir to combine. Brush the asparagus with the combined oils and sprinkle with the salt. Roast in the oven for 10 minutes, until just tender.

Transfer to a serving plate. Drizzle the reserved sauce evenly over the asparagus, sprinkle with the chives, and serve immediately.

Broccoli Rabe WITH PINE NUTS

Bitter greens are quite healthful, as that bitterness is the plant's defense against nibbling insects. It's also a clear sign of high antioxidant content, which is good news for humans who can acquire a taste for bitter foods. Broccoli rabe is on the mild end of the bitter spectrum, making it a good place to start. Although it appears similar to broccoli, broccolini, and Chinese broccoli, broccoli rabe is actually most closely related to turnips.

1½ pounds **broccoli rabe**

⅓ cup raw **pine nuts**

2 tablespoons extra-virgin **olive oil**

12 cloves **garlic**, peeled and thinly sliced

½ teaspoon **cayenne** (optional)

¼ cup dry **white wine**

1 tablespoon **balsamic vinegar**

½ teaspoon **sea salt**

Freshly ground **black pepper**

Fill a large saucepan with salted water and bring to a boil over high heat. Separate the stems of the broccoli rabe, trimming the stems as needed to make them equal in thicknesses. Add to the boiling water and stir. Drain in a colander.

Put the pine nuts and 1 tablespoon of the oil in a small skillet over medium-high heat. Shake the pan to keep the nuts moving until they have turned a light brown. Transfer to a plate lined with a folded paper towel. Blot any of the oil still clinging to the nuts with a separate paper towel. Transfer the nuts to a small bowl.

Put the remaining tablespoon of olive oil and the garlic and optional cayenne in a large skillet over medium-high heat. Swirl the pan to keep the garlic moving, separating the slices with a spoon as needed. As soon as the garlic begins to turn golden, add the broccoli rabe and stir constantly. When the skillet begins to dry out, add the wine and cover. When the hissing sound subsides, about 30 seconds, remove the cover and sprinkle the salt over the broccoli rabe. Cook until the broccoli rabe stems are just tender, 3 to 5 minutes. Remove from the heat, add the vinegar, and shake the pan to coat the broccoli rabe. Add the pine nuts, season with pepper to taste, and toss to distribute evenly. Serve immediately.

Roasted Broccolini WITH GARLIC AND LEMON

Roasting is such a popular method for cooking vegetables because it brings out their natural sweetness.

2 pounds **broccolini**

1 **lemon**

7 cloves **garlic**, thinly sliced

Freshly ground **black pepper**

Preheat the oven to 425 degrees F. Mist a baking sheet with olive oil spray.

Trim any coarse, tough portions of stem off the broccolini. If any stems are much thicker than others, slice them lengthwise to achieve uniformity as much as possible. Slice the lemon into ¼-inch-thick rounds and remove any seeds. Put the broccolini, lemon slices, and garlic in a large bowl. Mist lightly with olive oil spray and toss until evenly distributed. Mist and toss again.

Spread the broccolini, lemon, and garlic in a single layer on the prepared baking sheet. Roast in the oven for 4 minutes. Remove from the oven, season with pepper, and toss with a spatula or tongs. Return to the oven and roast for 3 minutes. Serve immediately.

Roasted Sweet Potatoes WITH FRAGRANT SPICES

Surprisingly, most people have only had sweet potatoes in a couple of ways—roasted, with butter and salt, and French-fried. This injustice is hereby corrected.

3 pounds **sweet potatoes**

1 cup unsweetened **almond milk**

1 tablespoon **pumpkin pie spice** blend

½ teaspoon **sea salt**

Preheat the oven to 400 degrees F. Line a baking sheet with foil.

Put the sweet potatoes on the prepared baking sheet and bake for 2 hours. Let cool completely. Peel the sweet potatoes and trim away any burned bits. Cut into bite-size pieces.

Put the almond milk, spice blend, and salt in a large saucepan over medium heat and cook, stirring constantly, until it is reduced to a sauce, 5 to 10 minutes. Add the sweet potato pieces and stir gently until they are coated with the sauce and warmed through. Serve immediately.

Mushrooms and Onions

MAKES 4 SERVINGS

There are few combinations more timeless or delicious than mushrooms and onions. Served on the side, this mix will work in concert with any savory dish. It also makes a tantalizing topping for veggie burgers or any warm sandwich filling served on a bun.

2 **red onions**, quartered and cut into ¼-inch-thick slices

2 pounds **button** or **brown mushrooms**, cut into ¼-inch-thick slices

¼ cup unsalted **vegetable broth**

1 teaspoon freshly squeezed **lemon juice**

¼ cup snipped **chives**

Freshly ground **black pepper**

Place a large sauté pan over medium-high heat until hot. Mist the pan with olive oil spray and immediately add the onions. Cook, stirring frequently, until the onions are soft and beginning to brown, about 7 minutes. Add the mushrooms and stir to combine with the onions. Decrease the heat to medium and cover the pan. Cook for 5 minutes, then remove the cover. If the mushrooms have begun to release their liquid, increase the heat to medium-high. If they haven't, replace the cover and cook for another 2 to 3 minutes, or until the juices run. Cook, stirring occasionally, until the onions and mushrooms have browned evenly. Add the broth and shake the pan to incorporate. As soon as the broth has reduced slightly, forming a light sauce, remove from the heat and stir in the lemon juice and half the chives. Shake the pan to incorporate. Season with pepper to taste. Garnish with the remaining chives and serve immediately.

Roasted Peppers and Onions

This multipurpose condiment is delicious either hot or cold. It can be a side dish, but it also brightens up sandwiches, salads, and vegetable dishes.

1 (16-ounce) jar **roasted red peppers**, drained and rinsed

2 **onions**, halved and cut into ¼-inch-thick slices

7 cloves **garlic**, thinly sliced (optional)

Freshly ground **black pepper**

Remove any seeds and blackened skins from the peppers. Cut the peppers crosswise into ¼-inch-thick strips.

Place a large sauté pan over medium-high heat. When hot, mist with olive oil spray and add the onions. Cook and stir until the onions begin to soften, about 4 minutes. Add the optional garlic and continue cooking, stirring frequently, until the onions are soft. Add the peppers and cook, stirring constantly, until the vegetables are nearly dry, 2 to 3 minutes. Season with pepper to taste. Remove from the heat and serve immediately. Alternatively, let cool, transfer to a clean glass jar, and refrigerate until cold. Stored in a sealed glass jar in the refrigerator, the peppers and onions will keep for up to one week.

11

Salads and Dressings

Grape Tomato and Hearts of Palm Salad

This incredibly simple salad is sublimely delicious.

3 cups **grape tomatoes**, cut in half crosswise

3 cups **hearts of palm**, drained, dried, and sliced ¼-inch thick (see tip)

¾ cup **Basil Cream Dressing** (page 103)

4 large **basil leaves**

Freshly ground **black pepper**

Put the tomatoes and hearts of palm in a medium bowl. Add the Basil Cream Dressing and stir gently until evenly distributed. Stack the basil leaves and slice them crosswise into thin strips. Fluff gently to separate the slices.

Divide the salad among four serving plates. Garnish with the basil strips and pepper. Serve immediately.

> **TIP** Heart of palm is a low-fat white vegetable obtained from the center of specific varieties of palm tree. It's prized for its culinary versatility and high polyphenol antioxidant content. Although it's most commonly added to salads, heart of palm can also be eaten on its own or even used as a vegan meat replacement. It has a slight crunch reminiscent of white asparagus, but its flavor is closer to that of artichoke hearts. Hearts of palm can be found jarred or canned in most supermarkets.

Kale Caesar Salad

This simple salad is packed with protein and antioxidants. It can stand on its own as a light meal or as a tasty complement to a soup or main dish.

3 cups stemmed and coarsely chopped **curly kale**, lightly packed

⅔ cup **Vegan Caesar Dressing** (page 108)

⅓ cup **nutritional yeast flakes**

¼ cup raw **walnuts** or **sunflower seeds**

¼ teaspoon **sea salt**

¾ cup unsalted cooked or canned **chickpeas**, rinsed and drained

Put the kale in a large bowl and add 3 tablespoons of the dressing. Toss until evenly distributed. Set aside for 20 minutes to let the kale soften.

Put the nutritional yeast, walnuts, and salt in a food processor and pulse just until the walnuts are coarsely chopped. Set aside.

Add the remaining dressing to the kale and toss until evenly distributed. Add the chickpeas and toss briefly, just until evenly distributed. To serve, divide equally among three large plates and sprinkle with the nutritional yeast mixture. Alternatively, put the salad in a serving dish and pass the nutritional yeast mixture at the table.

Black Bean and Corn Salad

What a feast for the eyes and palate! The mix of colors, textures, and flavors in this salad are impressive. In fact, this dish is so filling it could be served as the centerpiece of a meal.

2 cups frozen **white corn**

1 (25-ounce) can no-salt-added **black beans**, rinsed and drained

2 cups **grape tomatoes**, halved crosswise

I small **red onion**, finely diced

2 firm, ripe **avocados**, cut into ½-inch pieces

1½ cups packed coarsely chopped **fresh cilantro**

⅓ cup freshly squeezed **lime juice**

1 or 2 canned **chipotle chiles**, minced

¼ teaspoon freshly ground **black pepper** (optional)

Fill a medium saucepan with water and bring to a boil over high heat. Add the corn, stir, and cook until just tender, 2 to 3 minutes. Drain in a large strainer and shake to release as much water as possible. Transfer the corn to a large bowl. Add the beans, tomatoes, onion, avocados, cilantro, lime juice, chiles, and optional pepper. Toss gently but thoroughly. Serve immediately or refrigerate until cold.

Grilled Corn, Red Pepper, and Avocado Salad

MAKES 4 SERVINGS

White corn is naturally sweeter and more tender than yellow corn, and its kernels are slightly smaller as well. When white corn hobnobs with creamy avocado and crisp red bell peppers, the visual appeal alone will whet your appetite. Add scallions, fresh herbs, and a heavenly dressing, and you will wonder where this salad has been all your life!

2 **avocados**, peeled, seeded and cut into ½-inch dice

1 tablespoon freshly squeezed **lime juice**

4 ears **white corn**, shucked

2 **red bell peppers**, diced

1 bunch (about 12) **scallions**, white and green parts, thinly sliced

½ cup **cilantro**, coarsely chopped

1 cup **Avocado-Lime Dressing** (page 107)

Heat a grill until hot (see tip).

Immediately after dicing the avocados, put them in a medium bowl and add the lime juice. Toss gently to coat.

Place the corn on the grill. Cook until charred, turning as needed to char it evenly. Remove from the grill and wrap in foil, crimping to seal. Set aside and let the corn continue cooking in the residual heat.

When the corn is cool enough to handle, remove the foil and cut the kernels off the cobs over a large bowl so they fall into the bowl. Add the avocados, bell peppers, scallions, half the cilantro, and all the dressing. Toss gently but thoroughly, taking care not to mash the avocados.

Divide among four shallow bowls. Garnish with the remaining cilantro and serve immediately.

TIP If you don't have a grill or grill pan, you can broil the corn. Move the oven rack to the highest position (adjusting it as needed depending on the thickness of the corn) and preheat the broiler for 5 to 10 minutes. Line a baking sheet with foil. Place the corn on the lined baking sheet, mist lightly with olive oil spray, and broil until browned on all sides. Proceed with the recipe as directed. Alternatively, you can boil the corn in a large pot of water for 3 minutes. Drain well, let the corn cool, and proceed with the recipe as directed.

Cauli-Tabouli

Grated cauliflower stands in for bulgur in this gluten-free, oil-free, all-vegetable version of tabouli.

½ cup finely grated **cauliflower**

3 cups chopped **curly parsley**, packed

7 **scallions**, sliced or chopped

2 **Roma tomatoes**, seeded and diced

2 tablespoons freshly squeezed **lemon juice**

¼ teaspoon **sea salt**

Freshly ground **black pepper**

Fill a small saucepan halfway with water and bring to a boil over high heat. Add the cauliflower and cook for 2 minutes. Drain in a strainer and refresh under cold running water. Spread out on a folded paper towel and blot dry. Put the cauliflower in a medium bowl and add the parsley, scallions, tomatoes, lemon juice, and salt. Stir gently until well combined. Season with pepper to taste and stir until evenly distributed. Serve immediately.

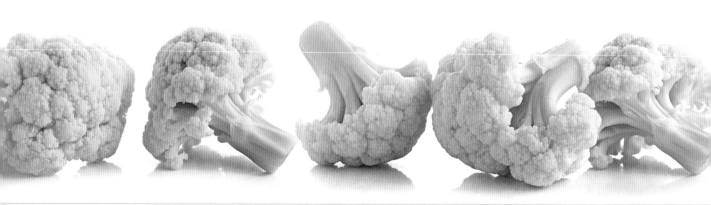

Curried Coleslaw

Every bite of this light slaw is bursting with unexpected flavor.

- 4 cups very thinly sliced or shredded **red cabbage**
- 2 stalks **celery**, halved lengthwise and thinly sliced diagonally
- 1 **fennel bulb**, cored and thinly sliced
- 1 **carrot**, grated
- 2 teaspoons **sea salt**
- ½ teaspoon **celery seeds**
- 2 tablespoons plain **rice vinegar**
- 2 teaspoons **curry powder**
- 1 teaspoon **ground ginger**
- ¼ teaspoon freshly ground **black pepper**
- ⅛ teaspoon **cayenne**

Put the cabbage, celery, fennel, and carrot in a large bowl. Add the salt and celery seeds and toss to combine. Let sit at room temperature until wilted, about 1 hour. Pour off the liquid.

Put the vinegar, curry powder, ginger, pepper, and cayenne in a large bowl and whisk to combine. Add the drained vegetable mixture and toss until evenly combined. Cover and refrigerate until ready to serve.

Coleslaw WITH SAVORY PEANUT DRESSING

If you have a food processor with a shredding disc, you can make fast work of the vegetables for this delectable salad.

- ¼ cup unsweetened, no-salt-added smooth **peanut butter**
- 2 tablespoons freshly squeezed **lime juice**
- 2 tablespoons low-sodium **soy sauce**
- 2 tablespoons plain **rice vinegar**
- 2 teaspoons **sriracha sauce**, or ¼ teaspoon **cayenne**
- ¼ teaspoon **garlic powder**
- ¼ teaspoon **ground ginger**
- ½ small **red cabbage**, shredded
- ½ small **green cabbage**, shredded
- 2 large **carrots**, peeled and shredded
- 1 small **red onion**, shredded (optional)
- 1 cup chopped **fresh cilantro** or **parsley**, packed

To make the dressing, put the peanut butter, lime juice, soy sauce, vinegar, sriracha sauce, garlic powder, and ginger in a small bowl. Stir until smooth and well combined. Set aside.

Put the purple cabbage, green cabbage, carrots, optional onion, and cilantro in a large bowl and toss to combine. Add the dressing and toss until evenly distributed. Serve immediately.

> TIP The salad and dressing can be prepared in advance and stored in separate sealed containers in the refrigerator. They will each keep for up to three days. Toss the salad and dressing together just before serving.

Chickpea, Tomato, and Cucumber Salad

Refreshing as well as satisfying, this salad is especially welcome in summer but can be enjoyed year round.

1 (15-ounce) can no-salt-added **chickpeas**, drained and rinsed

1½ cups **cherry tomatoes**, cut in half

1 seedless **cucumber**, diced

1 **green bell pepper**, diced

8 **scallions**, sliced

2 tablespoons coarsely chopped **fresh parsley**

¼ cup freshly squeezed **lemon juice**

2 cloves **garlic**, pressed

¼ teaspoon **sea salt**

6 tablespoons **tahini**

To make the salad, put the chickpeas, tomatoes, cucumber, bell pepper, scallions, and 1 tablespoon of the parsley in a large bowl and toss until well combined.

To make the dressing, put the lemon juice, garlic, and salt in a small bowl and whisk to combine. Add the tahini, 1 tablespoon at a time, whisking to blend after each addition. Add a little water, if needed, to achieve a creamy sauce. Pour over the salad and toss until evenly distributed.

Serve in small bowls or on lettuce leaves. Garnish with remaining tablespoon of parsley.

> TIP Seedless cucumbers, also known as English or hothouse cucumbers, are long and thin compared to standard cucumbers and have a tender, more delicate skin.

Beet and Cabbage Salad WITH PINK PEPPERCORNS

Despite their moniker, pink peppercorns, also known as Peruvian peppercorns, aren't actually pepper-corns at all; they are dried berries from a tree. Somewhat similar in shape and flavor to true pepper-corns, these fragrant berries have a delicate sweet-and-spicy flavor reminiscent of a mild citrus zest. You're sure to flip for this simple yet captivating combo.

½ head **red cabbage**, thinly sliced

½ pound **red beets**, grated

½ small **red onion**, thinly sliced

1 **orange**

½ teaspoon crushed **pink peppercorns**

Put the cabbage, beets, and onion in a medium bowl and toss until well combined. Zest the orange over the bowl. Squeeze the orange over the salad through a coarse strainer to catch any seeds. Press down on the pulp with a metal spatula to extract any remaining juice. Sprinkle the crushed peppercorns over the salad mixture and toss until evenly distributed. Serve immediately.

Pomegranate-Orange Salad

Enjoy this classic orange salad, which has extra zip from the addition of pomegranate seeds and pistachios.

6 **Valencia oranges**

¼ teaspoon **ground cinnamon**

1 cup **pomegranate arils**

1 tablespoon coarsely chopped **pistachios**

Mint leaves, torn or coarsely chopped (optional)

Peel the oranges, taking care to remove all of the pith. Cut them crosswise into slices a little thicker than ¼ inch. The goal is to have slices that don't break or fall apart. Pick out and discard any seeds. Try to capture any juices that run during the process. Arrange the slices on plates. Drizzle any captured juices over the slices. Sprinkle lightly with the cinnamon. Scatter the pomegranate arils and pistachios evenly over the oranges. Garnish with the optional mint leaves and serve immediately.

Basil Cream Dressing

This thick and luscious oil-free dressing is wonderful over steamed fingerling or baby potatoes as well as baked sweet potatoes and steamed broccoli, kale, or green beans. Of course, it's also delicious as a straightforward salad dressing on sturdier salad greens and vegetables.

½ cup raw **cashews** or blanched raw **almonds** (see tip), soaked in water for 8 to 12 hours, rinsed and drained

½ cup **water**

½ cup stemmed **fresh basil leaves**, firmly packed

Put the cashews and fresh water in a blender and process until smooth. Add the basil and process until smooth. Use immediately or cover tightly and store in the refrigerator for up to four days.

> **VARIATION:** To speed up the process, omit soaking the cashews for 8 to 12 hours. Instead, put cashews in a heatproof bowl, cover them with boiling water, and let soak for 1 hour. Drain and rinse the cashews and proceed with the recipe as directed.

> TIP Blanched raw almonds, also called peeled or skinless almonds, can be found in most supermarkets and natural food stores.

Creamy Herb Dressing

Herbs are fun and easy to grow at home, and you can have an assortment growing at once. If you don't have access to homegrown herbs, check out what's available at your local farmers market or grocery store. With so many varieties of herbs, this dressing offers endless variety.

½ cup raw **cashews** or blanched raw **almonds** (see tip), soaked in water for 8 to 12 hours, rinsed and drained

½ cup **water**

3 tablespoons plain **rice vinegar** or **white balsamic vinegar**

½ cup **fresh herbs**, such as basil, cilantro, parsley, mint, chives, thyme, savory, or chervil, lightly packed

Freshly ground **black pepper**

Put the cashews, fresh water, and vinegar in a blender and process until smooth. Add the fresh herbs and process until smooth. Season with pepper to taste and process briefly, just until incorporated. Use immediately or cover tightly and store in the refrigerator for up to four days.

VARIATION: To speed up the process, omit soaking the cashews for 8 to 12 hours. Instead, put cashews in a heatproof bowl, cover them with boiling water, and let soak for 1 hour. Drain and rinse the cashews and proceed with the recipe as directed.

TIP Blanched raw almonds, also called peeled or skinless almonds, can be found in most supermarkets and natural food stores.

Spicy Peanut Dip and Dressing

You'll find plenty of uses for this versatile dip and dressing, which is as equally at home on steamed veggies as it is on a baked potato or salad. For chopped salads, a thicker dressing is ideal. For leafy salads, a thinner dressing works best. Because it's loaded with flavor, just a little goes a long way!

2 **shallots**, peeled and thinly sliced

2 tablespoons minced **garlic**

¾ cup unsalted plain dry-roasted **peanuts**

⅓ cup **coconut milk**

1 tablespoon low-sodium **tamari**

Zest and juice of 1 **lime**

1 teaspoon **smoked paprika**

1 teaspoon **cayenne**

Put a large skillet over high heat until hot. Mist the skillet with olive oil spray and immediately put the shallots in the skillet, spreading the slices into a single layer. Cook until lightly browned, about 2 minutes. Turn the slices over and cook until just tender, 2 to 3 minutes. Add the garlic and cook, stirring constantly, until the garlic is very fragrant, about 2 minutes. Transfer to a blender and add the peanuts, coconut milk, tamari, lime zest and juice, smoked paprika, and cayenne. Process until smooth. For dressing, add ¼ cup of water. For a thinner dressing, add more water, 1 teaspoon at a time, until the desired consistency is achieved.

Roasted Red Pepper Dressing

Roasted peppers make a quick base for oil-free salad dressings. For this version, their rich flavor is enhanced with garlic, smoked paprika, and optional cayenne.

2 **roasted red bell peppers**, rinsed and patted dry

¼ cup raw **pine nuts**

¼ cup **water**

3 tablespoons **red wine vinegar**

2 cloves **garlic**

2 teaspoons **smoked paprika**

¼ teaspoon **cayenne** (optional)

¼ teaspoon **sea salt**

Remove and discard any seeds from the peppers and put the peppers in a blender. Add the pine nuts, water, vinegar, garlic, smoked paprika, optional cayenne, and salt, and process until smooth. Use at once or transfer to a jar, cover tightly, and store in the refrigerator for up to one week.

> TIP Jarred roasted bell peppers can be found in most supermarkets and natural food stores.

Avocado-Lime Dressing

Tart and creamy, this dressing has a smoky-hot tang that will enliven any salad, no matter how plain or fancy.

3 **limes**

Apple cider vinegar, as needed

3 cloves **garlic**, pressed or minced

½ teaspoon **smoked paprika**

½ teaspoon **cayenne**

½ teaspoon freshly ground **black pepper** (optional)

1 **avocado**, peeled and seeded

Zest the limes onto a small plate. Squeeze the limes over a measuring cup to catch the juice. Add apple cider vinegar, if needed, to make ⅓ cup. Transfer to a blender. Add the garlic, smoked paprika, cayenne, optional pepper, and avocado and process until smooth. Add water, 1 tablespoon at a time, if needed, to achieve the desired consistency. Transfer to a jar and stir in the lime zest. Cover tightly and refrigerate until needed. The dressing is best used the same day.

Vegan Caesar Salad Dressing

Though ideal for tossing with Kale Caesar Salad, page 90, this dressing is also delightful over torn romaine hearts or other sturdy lettuce combined with sliced red radishes. You can also use the dressing as a dip for carrot and celery sticks.

½ cup mashed **soft tofu**

1 tablespoon freshly squeezed **lemon juice**

1 tablespoon mellow **white miso**

1 tablespoon **Dijon mustard**

2 teaspoons **garlic powder**

2 teaspoons **apple cider vinegar**

½ teaspoon freshly ground **black pepper**

¼ teaspoon **sea salt**

Put all the ingredients in a high-speed blender and process until smooth. Stored in a covered container in the refrigerator, the dressing will keep for four days.

Balsamic-Almond Dressing

Simple, creamy, and just a wee bit sweet from the balsamic vinegar, this oil-free dressing is phenomenal on raw or cooked veggies as well as salads of every ilk.

⅓ cup blanched **almonds**

½ cup **balsamic vinegar**

1 tablespoon **Dijon mustard**

2 cloves **garlic** (optional)

Freshly ground **black pepper**

Put the almonds in a small heatproof bowl and pour boiling water over them to cover by 1 inch. Let sit until cooled. Drain, rinse, and drain again. Transfer the almonds to a blender and add the vinegar, mustard, and optional garlic. Process until smooth, adding water, 1 tablespoon at a time, until thin enough to pour a thin stream. Season with pepper to taste. Transfer to a glass jar and refrigerate. Stored in a sealed glass jar in the refrigerator, the dressing will keep for up to one week.

Sesame Dressing

This thick, creamy, healthful dressing is typically used with chopped vegetable salads, as it would over-whelm delicate lettuces. It can also double as a flavorful dip.

¼ cup grated **carrot**

¼ cup grated **daikon radish**

¼ cup chopped **sweet onion** (such as Maui or Vidalia)

¼ cup raw **sesame seeds**

¼ cup **rice vinegar**

¼ cup **water**

1 tablespoon low-sodium **soy sauce**

2 cloves **garlic**

¼ teaspoon **sea salt**

Put all the ingredients in a blender and process until smooth. Use immediately.

> **TIP** Although the dressing will keep for a few days in the refrigerator, it's best used shortly after it has been made, as the fresh vegetables will diminish in flavor somewhat when stored.

CHAPTER 12

Dips, Spreads, Sauces, Snacks, and Extras

Baba Ghanoush

Similar to hummus, baba ghanoush is made from roasted or grilled eggplant instead of chickpeas. Like hummus, it's delicious with pita bread and fresh veggies, but its silky texture and irresistible smoky flavor set it apart.

1 large **eggplant**

½ cup **tahini**

¼ cup freshly squeezed **lemon juice**

4 cloves **garlic**, crushed and chopped

Move the oven rack to a position that will accommodate the eggplant just below the broiler. Preheat the broiler on high and line a baking sheet with foil.

Put the eggplant on the lined baking sheet and place under the broiler. Broil until the eggplant's skin is charred, then turn the eggplant as needed and broil the remaining areas of skin. Remove the eggplant from the oven and wrap it tightly in foil.

Adjust the oven rack so it's in the middle of the oven. Change the setting from broil to bake at 400 degrees F. Return the eggplant to the oven and bake for 45 minutes, or until very tender. Remove from the oven and let cool.

Unwrap the eggplant and remove as much of the skin as possible. Transfer the eggplant and any juices to a food processor. Add the tahini, lemon juice, and garlic and process until smooth.

Classic Hummus

1 (15-ounce) can no-salt-added **chickpeas**, rinsed and drained

¼ cup freshly squeezed **lemon juice**, plus more as needed

2 cloves **garlic**, or ¼ teaspoon **garlic powder**

¼ cup **tahini**

2 tablespoons cold **water**

Sea salt

Cayenne or **crushed red pepper flakes** (optional)

Hot, **smoked**, or **regular paprika**, for garnish

Chopped **fresh parsley** or **dried oregano**, for garnish

Put the chickpeas, lemon juice, and garlic in a food processor and process until smooth. With the motor running, add the tahini, 1 tablespoon at a time, and the cold water. If the mixture is thin, add more tahini, 1 teaspoon at a time. If the mixture is too thick, thin it with a little more lemon juice or cold water, 1 teaspoon at a time. Season with salt and optional cayenne to taste.

To serve, spread in a wide, flat dish or platter. Garnish with paprika and parsley. Stored in a sealed container in the refrigerator, the hummus will keep for about one week.

AVOCADO HUMMUS: Add 1 ripe avocado along with the chickpeas.

BEET HUMMUS: Add ½ cup diced canned beets and 1 teaspoon dried dill weed along with the chickpeas.

HERB-INFUSED HUMMUS: Add 1 cup fresh herbs, such as basil, chives, cilantro, dill, or parsley (or a combination) along with the chickpeas. Omit the paprika and parsley and garnish with additional fresh herbs.

HUMMUS WITH A KICK: Add 1 jalapeño chile (remove seeds if you prefer less heat) along with the chickpeas.

KALAMATA OLIVE HUMMUS: Add ½ cup pitted kalamata olives along with the chickpeas.

ROASTED RED PEPPER HUMMUS: Add 2 jarred roasted red peppers, drained and seeded, along with the chickpeas.

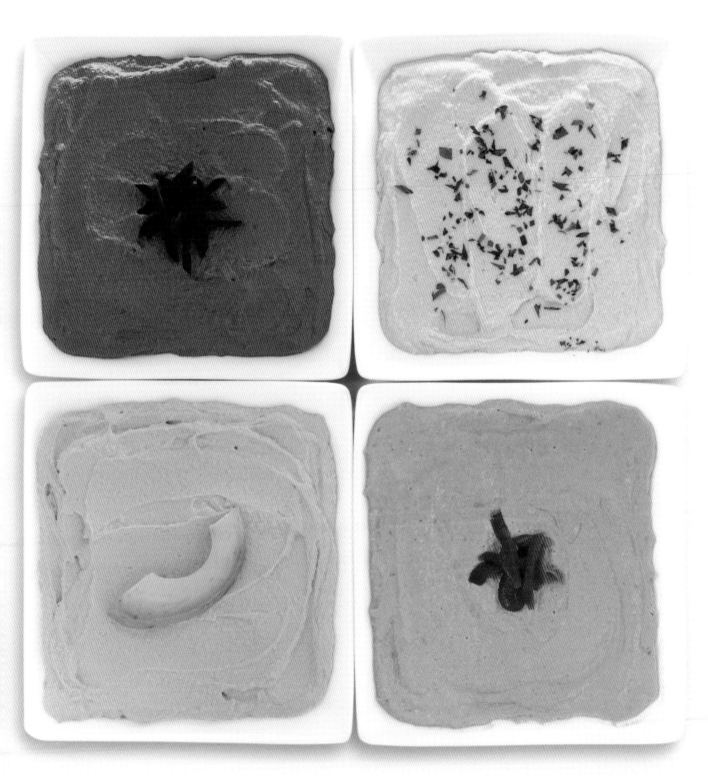

Black Bean Hummus

This pleasing twist on standard hummus is simple, smoky, and irresistible.

1 (15-ounce) **can** no-salt-added **black beans**, rinsed and drained

¼ cup freshly squeezed **lime juice**, plus more as needed

1 tablespoon **hot smoked paprika** or **smoked paprika** plus a pinch of **cayenne**

2 cloves **garlic**, or ¼ teaspoon **garlic powder**

½ cup **tahini**

¼ cup cold **water**

Sea salt

Chopped **fresh cilantro**, for garnish

Put the black beans, lime juice, smoked paprika, and garlic in a food processor and process until smooth. With the motor running, add the tahini, 1 tablespoon at a time, and the cold water. If the mixture is thin, add more tahini, 1 teaspoon at a time. If the mixture is too thick, thin it with a little more lime juice or cold water, 1 teaspoon at a time. Season with salt to taste.

To serve, spread in a wide, flat dish or platter. Garnish with cilantro. Stored in a sealed container in the refrigerator, the hummus will keep for about one week.

Edamame Hummus

This version of hummus brings the venerated dip into the twenty-first century with a fresh, exciting update. Wasabi, also known as Japanese horseradish, is a pungent green paste typically served as a condiment with sushi. It is rich in antioxidants and will add a burst of unexpected flavor to this unique spread.

1 pound frozen **edamame**

¼ cup freshly squeezed **lemon juice**, plus more as needed

1 tablespoon prepared **wasabi** (optional)

2 cloves **garlic**, or ¼ teaspoon **garlic powder**

½ cup **tahini**

¼ cup cold **water**

Sea salt

Black or white **sesame seeds**, for garnish

Fill a medium saucepan with water and bring to a boil over high heat. Add the edamame and stir. Cook for 3 minutes. Drain the edamame in a strainer and rinse under cold running water until cooled.

Put the edamame, lemon juice, optional wasabi, and garlic in a food processor and process until smooth. With the motor running, add the tahini, 1 tablespoon at a time, and the cold water. If the mixture is thin, add more tahini, 1 teaspoon at a time. If the mixture is too thick, thin it with a little more lemon juice or cold water, 1 teaspoon at a time. Season with salt to taste.

To serve, spread in a wide, flat dish or platter. Garnish with sesame seeds. Stored in a sealed container in the refrigerator, the hummus will keep for about one week.

> TIP Wasabi is available as a powder in most natural food stores, so if you can't find the paste locally, you can make your own from the powder.

Walnut Dip and Sandwich Spread

Walnuts are the only nuts that contain omega-3 fatty acids, which are both essential and anti-inflammatory. Soaking walnuts prior to using them helps to remove the bitterness from the skin. Serve this flavor-packed dip with carrot and celery sticks or use it as a sandwich spread.

2 medjool **dates**, pitted

2 cups **walnuts**

1 large **tomato**, coarsely chopped

⅓ cup **fresh parsley leaves**

4 cloves **garlic**, minced or pressed

1 teaspoon **paprika**

1 teaspoon **cayenne**

Put the dates in a small heatproof bowl. Cover with boiling water and let soak until cool. Drain thoroughly.

Put the walnuts in a medium heatproof bowl, cover with boiling water, and let soak until cool. Drain thoroughly. Put the walnuts, dates, tomato, parsley, garlic, paprika, and cayenne in a food processor and process until finely ground. Add water, 1 tablespoon at a time, as needed to achieve the desired consistency. Transfer to a bowl and cover tightly. Let sit at room temperature for about 1 hour before serving to allow the flavors to develop. Stored in a sealed container in the refrigerator, the dip will keep for up to two days.

Artichoke Dip and Sandwich Spread

An artichoke bottom is the fleshy base of the artichoke's leaves. The bottoms have a tender texture and flavorful taste, similar to artichoke hearts.

¼ cup raw **cashews**

1 (13.75-ounce) can **artichoke bottoms**

¼ cup coarsely chopped **parsley**, lightly packed

1 tablespoon freshly squeezed **lemon juice**

1 tablespoon **capers**, rinsed and drained

2 cloves **garlic**, minced or pressed

Freshly ground **black pepper**

Put the cashews in a small heatproof bowl. Cover with boiling water and let soak until cool. Drain, rinse under cold water, and drain again. Drain and rinse the artichokes. Spread them out on a towel and pat dry.

Put the cashews, artichoke bottoms, parsley, lemon juice, capers, and garlic in a food processor and pulse until chunky (the artichoke bottoms should be in about ¼-inch pieces). Season with pepper to taste. Transfer to a bowl and cover tightly. Let sit at room temperature for 1 hour to allow the flavors to develop. Stored in a sealed container in the refrigerator, the dip will keep for up to two days.

Kale Chips

This delicious, crunchy treat is a breeze to prepare, and because it's so tasty, it seems more like a snack than a serving of vegetables.

1 large bunch **curly kale**, stemmed and torn into 2-inch pieces

2 teaspoons extra-virgin **olive oil**

Sea salt

Preheat the oven to 300 degrees F. Line two sheet pans with parchment paper.

Rinse the kale and dry it thoroughly in a salad spinner or by rolling up the leaves in towels. Transfer to a large bowl and drizzle the oil over the top. Sprinkle lightly with salt and toss until the kale is evenly coated.

Divide the kale between the prepared sheet pans, spreading it out evenly. Bake for 10 to 15 minutes, or until crisp.

VARIATION: Leave the kale slightly moist to help seasonings adhere. After the kale is tossed with the oil and salt, add one of the following options:

- 1 to 3 tablespoons nutritional yeast flakes
- 2 tablespoons nutritional yeast flakes plus 1 teaspoon smoked paprika
- 1 to 2 teaspoons curry powder

Tahini Sauce, Dressing, and Dip

MAKES ABOUT 1½ CUPS

This sauce is quite adaptable. It's fantastic over broccoli and dark leafy greens (chard, collard greens, kale, spinach), whole grains, beans, and even pasta. It makes a delicious salad dressing, and with less water, it turns into a simple yet rich dip for raw or steamed vegetables. It also is a good base to create more intricate sauces and dressings by adding fresh herbs (basil, cilantro, dill, parsley) or your favorite seasonings.

1 cup **water**, plus more as needed

½ cup **tahini**

2 tablespoons freshly squeezed **lemon juice**, plus more as needed

2 cloves **garlic**

½ teaspoon **sea salt**

Put all the ingredients in a high-speed blender and process until smooth. If the sauce is too thick, add more lemon juice or water, 1 tablespoon at a time, and process until incorporated. Stored in a sealed container in the refrigerator, the sauce will keep for up to one week.

Basil Pesto

MAKES 1 CUP

Pesto is terrific tossed with pasta, but it also adds an extra layer of flavor when stirred into soups or blended into mashed potatoes instead of butter. Because it's so rich and flavorful, a little goes a long way.

1 cup **fresh basil leaves**, firmly packed

¼ cup **macadamia nuts**

1 clove **garlic**, minced or pressed

¼ teaspoon **sea salt**

Freshly ground **black pepper**

Put the basil, macadamia nuts, garlic, and salt in a food processor and process until smooth. Season with pepper to taste. Alternatively, process with a hand-held immersion blender.

Cilantro Pesto

Cilantro pesto makes a great sauce for zucchini noodles (also known as zoodles). You can also use it as a sandwich filling, as a replacement for tomato sauce on pizza, as a dressing for a fresh tomato salad, or as a topping for a baked potato. The possibilities are endless!

2 cups **fresh cilantro leaves**, firmly packed

½ cup raw **sunflower seeds**, **pumpkin seeds**, **pine nuts**, or **walnuts**

2 tablespoons freshly squeezed **lime juice**

1 **jalapeño chile**, sliced (remove seeds if you prefer less heat)

1 clove **garlic**

½ teaspoon **sea salt**

2 tablespoons **water**, plus more as needed

Put the cilantro, sunflower seeds, lime juice, chile, garlic, and salt in a food processor or blender (see tip). Process until smooth, stopping occasionally to scrape down the sides of the container. Add water, 1 tablespoon at a time, to achieve the desired consistency. Stored in a sealed container in the refrigerator, the pesto will keep for two days. Alternatively, store in the freezer for up to six months.

> TIP A food processor will give the pesto a bit of texture, whereas a blender will produce a smoother pesto.

Cilantro Chutney

If you enjoy blazing hot food, you've met your match. This is good on top of hummus-topped toast or in a salad.

1½ cups coarsely chopped **fresh cilantro leaves and tender stems**, packed

2 hot **green chiles** (remove seeds for less heat)

2 tablespoons chopped **red onion**

1 tablespoon peeled and chopped **fresh ginger**

1 tablespoon freshly squeezed **lemon** or **lime juice**

1 clove **garlic**

¼ teaspoon **sea salt**

Put all the ingredients in a high-speed blender and process until smooth. Add 1 tablespoon of water, if needed, to keep the mixture moving. Stop occasionally to scrape down the sides of the container. Serve immediately.

Pico de Gallo

Pico de gallo is a fresh, uncooked, chunky Mexican salsa that can be used as a condiment for burritos, tacos, and baked whole-grain tortilla chips. It's traditionally made with equal parts tomatoes and onion, along with fresh cilantro and a generous squeeze of lime juice. We add jalapeño for a spicy kick, but you can leave it out if you prefer a milder version.

3 **Roma tomatoes**, diced

1 **white** or **red onion**, diced

½ cup coarsely chopped **fresh cilantro**, packed

3 **jalapeño chiles**, diced

Juice of 1 **lime**

Put the tomatoes, onion, cilantro, and chiles in a medium bowl and toss until well combined. Add the lime juice and toss again until evenly distributed. Transfer to a small bowl and serve immediately.

Barbecue Sauce

Smoky but not packing too much heat, this barbecue sauce checks all the right boxes. Bonus? It takes mere minutes from start to finish.

1 cup low-sodium **ketchup** or no-salt-added **tomato purée**

¼ cup **water**

3 tablespoons freshly squeezed **lime juice**

2 **chipotle chiles** in adobo sauce (see tip)

1 tablespoon low-sodium **tamari**

4 cloves **garlic**

½ teaspoon **dry mustard**

½ teaspoon **smoked paprika**

½ teaspoon **celery seeds**

⅛ teaspoon **ground allspice**

Put all the ingredients in a blender and process until smooth. Add additional water, if needed, 1 tablespoon at a time. Scrape into a clean jar, cover tightly, and store in the refrigerator. Return to room temperature or heat before using.

> TIP Look for chipotle chiles in adobo sauce in the Mexican or international section of your grocery store.

Guacamole

As iconic in the quick-snack world as hummus, guacamole is an anti-inflammatory delight.

1 ripe **avocado**

⅓ cup coarsely chopped **fresh cilantro**

¼ cup diced **red** or **white onion**

1 tablespoon freshly squeezed **lime juice**

1 **serrano chile**, diced

Cut the avocado in half lengthwise, down to the pit. Separate the two halves and discard the pit. Scoop out the flesh and put it in a medium bowl. Mash the flesh coarsely, leaving a few small chunks. Add the cilantro, onion, lime juice, and chile and mix thoroughly. Transfer to a small bowl and serve immediately or cover tightly and refrigerate until ready to serve.

Pine Nut–Red Pepper Sauce

An explosion of flavor, this sauce will elevate anything you put it on. It makes a delectable dip for raw veggies, a compelling sauce for steamed or grilled veggies, and a phenomenal sandwich spread.

½ cup raw **pine nuts**

2 **roasted red bell peppers**, seeded, rinsed, and patted dry

1 tablespoon **smoked paprika**

1 tablespoon **red wine vinegar**

1 tablespoon no-salt-added **tomato paste**

4 cloves **garlic**

¼ teaspoon **cayenne**

¼ teaspoon **salt**

Mist a small skillet with olive oil spray and place over medium heat. Add the pine nuts and toast them until lightly browned, 2 to 3 minutes. Transfer to a high-speed blender and add the bell peppers, smoked paprika, vinegar, tomato paste, garlic, cayenne, and salt. Process until smooth. Add water, 1 tablespoon at a time, until the desired consistency is achieved. Stored in a sealed container in the refrigerator, the sauce will keep for up to one week.

Tempeh or Chickpea Croutons

These wholesome, high-fiber, crispy croutons are one of the most delicious and healthful ways to top a salad or bowl of soup.

8 ounces **tempeh**, or 1 (15-ounce) can no-salt-added **chickpeas**, rinsed and drained

Preheat the oven to 425 degrees F. Line a baking sheet with parchment paper or aluminum foil and lightly mist with olive oil spray.

For tempeh croutons, cut the tempeh into ¾-inch cubes. For chickpea croutons, put the chickpeas on a double thickness of paper towels and blot off any water.

Spread the tempeh or chickpeas in a single layer on the prepared baking sheet and lightly mist the tops with olive oil. Roast on the middle oven shelf for 10 to 15 minutes, until lightly browned and crisp but not hard. Let cool before serving.

> **VARIATION:** Put the tempeh cubes or chickpeas in a medium bowl and mist lightly with olive oil spray. Dust with smoked paprika, chili powder, dried herbs, or other seasonings that would complement the soup or salad you plan to use them with. Toss to coat and proceed with the recipe as directed.

Cheesy Sauce

You won't miss cheese one bit when you have this zesty sauce on hand. Drizzle it over baked tortilla chips, baked potato wedges, or steamed veggies (broccoli, cauliflower, kale, or Brussels sprouts). Stir it into hot elbow macaroni to make a speedy mac and cheese. Or spread it over whole-grain bread, Ezekiel bread, or multigrain tortillas. Add avocado slices, baby lettuce or sprouts, and sliced fresh tomatoes to make rave-worthy sandwiches or wraps.

½ cup raw **pumpkin seeds**, **sunflower seeds**, or **cashews**

2 large **roasted red peppers**, seeds removed (see tips)

⅓ cup **water**, plus more as needed

2 tablespoons **nutritional yeast flakes**

2 tablespoons freshly squeezed **lemon juice**, plain **rice vinegar**, or **apple cider vinegar**

1 tablespoon **sriracha sauce** or other hot sauce

1 teaspoon **smoked paprika**

1 teaspoon **garlic powder**

½ teaspoon **sea salt**, plus more as needed

Put all the ingredients in a high-speed blender and process until smooth. If the sauce is too thick, add a little more water, 1 teaspoon at a time, processing briefly after each addition until the desired consistency is achieved. Taste and add more salt if needed. Stored in a sealed container, the sauce will keep for up to five days in the refrigerator or up to three months in the freezer.

> **TIP** Jarred roasted red peppers are available at most supermarkets.

Cashew Crema

Typically used as a garnish or condiment for tacos and other Mexican fare, crema also adds a tangy bite to soups and vegetables. In addition, it makes an excellent replacement for crème fraîche, which is used similarly in French cuisine. Both crema and crème fraîche are slightly soured and thickened cream, milder and thinner than American sour cream. Just a small swirl, dollop, or drizzle per serving is all that's needed to tame spicy dishes or add a rich, creamy element.

½ cup **cashews**

   ½ cup **water**

   1 tablespoon freshly squeezed **lime juice**

Put the cashews and water in a blender and let sit for 15 minutes. Add the lime juice and process until smooth. Stored tightly covered in the refrigerator, the crema will keep for up to five days.

Date Paste

Date Paste is a thick, creamy, healthy natural sweetener. With only three ingredients, it's also quick and easy to prepare. Date Paste is the ideal replacement for refined sugar and can be used in a wide range of recipes. Dates are naturally sweet, rich in fiber, and packed with flavonoids known for their anti-inflammatory properties.

   1½ cups **water**

   1¼ cups pitted medjool or deglet noor **dates**

   1 teaspoon freshly squeezed **lemon juice**

Put all the ingredients in a high-speed blender and process until smooth. Stored in a sealed glass jar in the refrigerator, Date Paste will keep for up to three weeks.

CHAPTER

13

Satisfying Main Dishes

Mushroom Fettuccine Alfredo

Surprisingly, it's quite easy to make sumptuous fettuccine Alfredo without any oil or dairy products.

8 ounces **fettuccine**, cooked according to package directions

1 cup raw **cashews**, soaked in hot water for 30 minutes and drained well

¾ cup unsweetened **almond milk** or **water**

2½ tablespoons freshly squeezed **lemon juice**

½ teaspoon **sea salt**

½ teaspoon freshly ground **black pepper**, plus more for garnish

¼ teaspoon **garlic powder**

¼ teaspoon **onion powder**

⅛ teaspoon **dried thyme**

Pinch **ground nutmeg**

1 cup sliced **mushrooms**

Fresh parsley leaves, for garnish

Put the cooked fettuccine in a large bowl and mist with olive oil spray to keep it from sticking. Toss gently to distribute the oil, misting the fettuccine again as needed. Cover the bowl and set aside.

To make the sauce, put the cashews, almond milk, lemon juice, salt, pepper, garlic powder, onion powder, thyme, and nutmeg in a high-speed blender and process until smooth and creamy. Set aside.

Mist a medium skillet with olive oil spray and place over medium-high heat. When hot, add the mushrooms, decrease the heat to medium, and cook, stirring occasionally, until the mushrooms are softened and lightly browned, 5 to 7 minutes. Remove from the heat and add the reserved sauce. Stir until the sauce is warmed through, pour over the fettuccine, and toss until evenly distributed. Garnish each serving with additional pepper and parsley.

> **VARIATION:** Omit the nutmeg and add a pinch of cayenne and/or a pinch of smoked paprika.

Fiery Pasta e Fagioli

Add more chile flakes if you like four-alarm heat, or omit them entirely if you prefer milder seasonings.

1 (25-ounce) can chopped **tomatoes**

7 cloves **garlic**, minced or pressed

1 teaspoon **crushed red chile flakes**

2 (15-ounce) cans no-salt-added **cannellini beans** or other **white beans**, rinsed and drained

Freshly ground **black pepper**

1 pound **brown rice pasta**, preferably penne or ziti

½ cup packed **fresh basil**, coarsely chopped

Put the tomatoes, garlic, and chile flakes in a medium saucepan and place over medium heat. Cook, stirring occasionally, until the tomatoes begin to break down and form a sauce, about 7 minutes. Add the beans and cook, stirring frequently, until warmed through, about 4 minutes. Season with pepper to taste.

Fill a large saucepan with water and bring to a boil over medium-high heat. Add the pasta and stir well to prevent sticking. Cook until the pasta is tender but still firm. Scoop out ½ cup of the cooking water and set aside. Drain the pasta in a colander and quickly transfer it to the saucepan with the sauce. Add the basil. Stir gently to coat the pasta. If the mixture seems dry, add the reserved cooking liquid and shake the saucepan to distribute it evenly. Serve immediately.

Spaghetti Seitanese

Twirl your fork around this deliciously inventive spin on traditional Italian Bolognese!

½ cup chopped **celery**

⅓ cup chopped **onion**

⅓ cup chopped **carrot**

8 ounces **Italian-flavor seitan crumbles**

½ cup unsweetened **almond milk**

1 cup no-salt-added canned crushed **tomatoes**

⅛ teaspoon **ground nutmeg**

Freshly **ground black pepper**

1 pound **spaghetti**

Place a medium saucepan over medium heat and mist with olive oil spray. Add the celery, onion, and carrot. Cook, stirring frequently, until the vegetables become aromatic, 10 to 15 minutes. Decrease the heat to medium-low, cover, and cook until the vegetables are tender, about 10 minutes. Add the seitan crumbles and stir until evenly distributed. Add the almond milk and stir until well combined. Cook, stirring occasionally, until the milk has been absorbed, about 10 minutes. Add the tomatoes and nutmeg and stir until well combined. Cook, stirring frequently, until the tomatoes have formed a delicate sauce, 15 to 20 minutes. Season with pepper to taste. Decrease the heat to low.

Fill a large saucepan with water and bring to a boil over medium-high heat. Add the spaghetti and cook according to the package directions or until just tender. Scoop out ⅓ cup of the cooking liquid and set aside. Drain the spaghetti in a colander and return it to the saucepan. Add the sauce and shake the saucepan to distribute it evenly with the spaghetti. If the sauce is very thick, add the reserved cooking water and shake the saucepan to combine it with the sauce and spaghetti. Serve immediately.

Veggie Pancakes

For a snack or light meal, these savory pancakes can't be beat. Chickpea flour, an essential ingredient, is available at natural food stores, Indian markets, and online. It's worth seeking out, even if you only use it for this recipe. Serve the pancakes with Pine Nut–Red Pepper Sauce (page 124) or Cilantro Chutney (page 122).

3 cups **chickpea flour**

1 tablespoon **smoked paprika**

1½ teaspoons **sea salt**

1¾ cups unsalted **vegetable broth**

1 large **onion**, quartered and thinly sliced

8 **scallions**, thinly sliced

2 cloves **garlic**, minced or pressed

2 small **zucchini**, quartered and thinly sliced

1 small **carrot**, grated

1 teaspoon **dried thyme**

2 tablespoons chopped **parsley**

Freshly ground **black pepper**

To make the batter, put the chickpea flour, smoked paprika, and salt in a medium bowl and stir with a dry whisk to combine. Slowly add the broth, whisking to break up any lumps. Whisk until smooth and slightly thickened. Cover tightly and refrigerate for at least 30 minutes or up to 12 hours.

Mist a large saucepan with olive oil spray and place over medium-high heat. When the pan is hot, add the onion, scallions, and garlic and cook, stirring frequently, until soft and golden, 10 to 12 minutes. Add the zucchini, carrot, and thyme and cook, stirring frequently, until soft, 12 to 15 minutes. Add water, 1 tablespoon at a time, if needed to prevent sticking. Remove from the heat, stir in the parsley, and season with pepper to taste. Add the vegetables to the batter and stir until evenly distributed.

Preheat the oven to 300 degrees F. Mist a nonstick skillet with olive oil spray and place over medium heat. Put ⅓ cup of batter into the skillet and cook until the pancake is lightly browned on the bottom, about 1½ minutes. Turn the pancake over and cook on the other side until lightly browned, about 1 minute. Transfer to a baking sheet and put in the oven to keep warm. Repeat with the remaining batter.

Artichoke and Bulgur Rolls

You'll never crave stuffed grape leaves again once you try these incomparable stuffed Swiss chard rolls. Serve them with Tahini Sauce (page 120) or Pine Nut-Red Pepper Sauce (page 124) on top or on the side, along with a light sprinkle of paprika or sumac for a gorgeous presentation.

1 cup **bulgur**

2 cups unsalted **vegetable broth**

⅓ cup **pine nuts**

2 large **shallots** or 1 small **onion**, finely diced

1 (14-ounce) can **artichoke bottoms**, drained, rinsed, and cut into bite-size pieces

¼ cup chopped **green olives**

¼ cup chopped **fresh mint** or **parsley**, lightly packed

4 large **Swiss chard** leaves

Put the bulgur and broth in a small saucepan over medium-high heat and bring to a boil. Cover, decrease the heat to medium-low, and cook for 12 minutes. If any liquid remains, cook, uncovered, 2 to 4 minutes longer, until nearly dry. Cover and set aside.

Toast the pine nuts in a small skillet over medium-high heat until lightly browned, 3 to 4 minutes. Transfer to a plate to cool.

Mist a medium pan with olive oil spray and place over medium-high heat. Add the shallots and cook, stirring frequently, until soft, 10 to 12 minutes. Add the artichokes and cook, stirring occasionally, until lightly browned, about 10 minutes. Remove from the heat and add the bulgur, pine nuts, olives, and mint. Stir well.

Fill a large bowl with cold water. Fill a large saucepan with water and bring to a boil over medium-high heat. Holding the chard by the stems, dip into the boiling water until limp, about 30 seconds. Immediately plunge the leaves into the cold water. Gently shake the chard over the sink to remove excess water, then blot the leaves dry with a towel. Lay the leaves on a work surface with the veins facing down. Cut off the stems. Divide the bulgur mixture equally among the leaves. Fold the sides of one of the leaves over the filling. Fold the stem end over the sides and then roll up into a cylinder. Repeat with the remaining leaves. Rinse out the saucepan. Place the rolls in the saucepan and sprinkle ¼ cup of water around them. Place the pan over medium-high heat. As soon as the water begins to boil, adjust the heat to maintain a simmer, cover the pan, and cook until the chard is tender, 10 to 15 minutes. Transfer the rolls to plates and serve immediately.

Aloo Gobi

The spices in this popular Indian dish elevate humble potatoes and cauliflower to great heights of flavor, along with an added boost of disease-fighting compounds. This dish is traditionally served with brown rice or whole wheat rotis.

2 **waxy potatoes**

1 large head **cauliflower**

1 tablespoon finely grated **fresh ginger**

2 teaspoons **ground coriander**

1 teaspoon **ground cumin**

½ teaspoon **sea salt**

¼ teaspoon **ground turmeric**

¼ teaspoon **cayenne**

⅓ cup **water**

2 tablespoons extra-virgin **olive oil**

¼ teaspoon **cumin seeds**

2 tablespoons coarsely chopped **fresh cilantro**, for garnish

Put the potatoes in a small saucepan, cover with water, and bring to a boil over medium-high heat. Adjust the heat to maintain a simmer and cook until the potatoes are just tender, 15 to 20 minutes. Drain and refresh in cold water. When the potatoes have cooled, peel and cut them into 1-inch dice. Separate the cauliflower into florets about 1½ inches wide.

Put the ginger, coriander, cumin, salt, turmeric, and cayenne in a small bowl. Add the water and stir to combine.

Put the oil in a large saucepan over medium-high heat. When hot, add the cumin seeds and swirl the saucepan. Cook until the cumin seeds release their aroma, 2 seconds. Add the potatoes and cauliflower and cook, stirring frequently, until the vegetables are browned, 10 to 12 minutes. Add the spice mixture and cook, stirring constantly, for 1 minute. Add ¼ cup of water, adjust the heat to maintain a simmer, and cook, stirring occasionally, until the vegetables are tender and the liquid has been absorbed, 3 to 5 minutes. Transfer to a serving dish, garnish with the cilantro, and serve immediately.

Stir-Fried Udon Noodles

Udon are thick, chewy wheat noodles used in Japanese cuisine. They hold up beautifully in a vegetable stir-fry, like this one, even when bathed in a tantalizing peanut sauce.

8 ounces **udon noodles**

2 teaspoons **toasted sesame oil**

⅓ cup unsweetened, no-salt-added **peanut butter**

¼ cup unsalted **vegetable broth** or **water**

1½ tablespoons low-sodium **soy sauce**

1½ tablespoons **rice vinegar**

2 teaspoons extra-virgin **olive oil**

1 small **carrot**, cut into matchsticks

1 **red bell pepper**, cut into thin strips

7 **scallions**, sliced on a sharp diagonal

¼ cup coarsely chopped **cilantro**, packed

1 **lime**, cut into wedges

Fill a large saucepan with water and bring to a boil over medium-high heat. Add the noodles gradually so the water doesn't stop boiling. Cook, stirring occasionally, until the noodles are just tender. Drain in a colander. Rinse the noodles well under cold running water, using your hands to help remove surface starch. Drain well and return to the saucepan. Add the toasted sesame oil and shake the saucepan to coat the noodles with it.

Put the peanut butter, broth, soy sauce, and vinegar in a small bowl and stir until well combined. If the mixture is very thick, add 1 or 2 tablespoons of water. It should be thick enough to coat a spoon.

Put the olive oil in a wok or large skillet over medium-high heat. Swirl wok to coat with the oil. When hot, add the carrot and red pepper. Cook, stirring briskly, until the vegetables are tender-crisp, 2 to 3 minutes. Add the scallions and cook, stirring constantly until just barely wilted, about 1 minute. Add the noodles and the peanut sauce. Toss gently until the sauce and vegetables are evenly combined with the noodles.

Divide the noodles and vegetables among four shallow bowls. Garnish with the cilantro and serve with the lime wedges.

Nourishing Vegetable Stew

Portobello mushrooms stand in for beef in this soothing, satisfying stew. Just add a tossed salad and dinner is served!

2 **yellow** or **white onions**, cut into ¾-inch chunks

3 **carrots**, sliced in half lengthwise and cut into ¾-inch pieces

3 ribs **celery**, cut into ¾-inch pieces

2 **portobello mushrooms**, cut into ¾-inch chunks

6 cloves **garlic**, minced or pressed

5 cups **water**

2 pounds **potatoes**, peeled and cut into ¾-inch chunks

6 tablespoons no-salt-added **tomato paste** (about half of a 6-ounce can)

1 tablespoon **dried Italian seasoning**

1 tablespoon **paprika**

½ teaspoon **dried rosemary**

1½ cups frozen **peas**, defrosted

½ cup chopped **fresh parsley**, lightly packed

Put 1 tablespoon of water in a large saucepan over medium-high heat. When the water starts to sputter, add the onions, carrots, and celery, and cook, stirring frequently, until the vegetables begin to soften, about 8 minutes. Add more water, 1 tablespoon at a time, as needed to prevent sticking.

Stir in the mushrooms and garlic, and cook, stirring constantly, until the mushrooms begin to release their juice, about 5 minutes. Add more water, 1 tablespoon at a time, as needed to prevent sticking.

Add the 5 cups of water, potatoes, tomato paste, Italian seasoning, paprika, and rosemary and bring to a boil. Decrease the heat to medium-low, cover, and cook, stirring occasionally, until the potatoes and carrots are very tender, 25 to 30 minutes. Add the peas and cook, stirring occasionally, until tender and hot, about 5 minutes.

Transfer 2 cups of the broth and vegetables to a blender and pulse or process briefly, just until smooth. Stir the mixture into the stew to create a thick gravy. Stir in the parsley and serve immediately.

Green Lentils WITH MUSTARD GREENS

In Middle Eastern cooking, lentils and greens are a recurring combination, and a winning one. Feel free to replace the mustard greens with other dark leafy greens. For a complete meal, serve this dish with your favorite whole grain.

12 ounces **French green lentils**

1 large **onion**, finely diced

3 tablespoons minced **garlic**

2 teaspoons **smoked paprika**

1 teaspoon **ground coriander**

1 teaspoon **ground cumin**

½ teaspoon freshly ground **black pepper**

1 pound **mustard greens**, coarsely chopped

Sea salt

½ cup coarsely chopped **fresh cilantro**, packed (optional)

1 tablespoon freshly squeezed **lemon juice**

Pick over the lentils to remove any small stones or other debris. Rinse well and place in a large, heavy saucepan. Add enough cold water to cover the lentils by about an inch and bring to a boil over medium-high heat. Add the onion, garlic, smoked paprika, coriander, cumin, and pepper. Adjust the heat to maintain a steady simmer and cook, stirring occasionally, for 15 minutes.

Stir in the mustard greens and cook until the lentils are tender and the liquid is reduced to a sauce, 5 to 10 minutes. Season with salt to taste and cook for 2 minutes longer. Remove from the heat, stir in the optional cilantro and lemon juice, and serve immediately.

Red Curry WITH BOK CHOY AND TOFU

MAKES 4 SERVINGS

The spices used by ancient cultures have always been as equally valued for their health-promoting properties as for their flavor. In this lovely curry, those qualities coincide in perfect harmony. To complete your meal, serve the curry on a bed of brown rice.

1 pound **firm tofu**, cut into bite-size cubes

1 tablespoon low-sodium **soy sauce**

2 large heads **bok choy**

¼ cup **water**

3 tablespoons **red curry paste**

2 cups light **coconut milk**

⅓ cup **basil leaves**, firmly packed

1 tablespoon freshly squeezed **lime juice**

4 **scallions**, thinly sliced on a sharp diagonal

Put the tofu in a shallow bowl. Drizzle with the soy sauce and gently toss until evenly coated.

Cut the bok choy crosswise into 1-inch pieces and coarsely chop the leaves. Transfer to a large saucepan, add the water, and place over medium-high heat. Cook, stirring constantly, until the bok choy is tender-crisp and the water has been absorbed, about 4 minutes. Add the curry paste and stir to incorporate. Add the coconut milk and stir until well combined. Increase the heat to high and cook, stirring constantly, until the mixture comes to a boil. Decrease the heat to medium, add the tofu, and cook just until it is warmed through.

Coarsely tear the basil leaves and add them to the saucepan. Stir gently to evenly distribute them, taking care not to break the tofu cubes. Remove from the heat and stir in the lime juice.

Spoon into serving bowls, garnish with the scallions, and serve immediately.

Cannellini WITH SWISS CHARD AND ROSEMARY

Beans and greens are a time-honored duo with understated charm. It's worth seeking out fresh rosemary, as it will enliven this dish even further.

2 large bunches **red** or **rainbow Swiss chard**

2 cups unsalted **vegetable broth**

7 cloves **garlic**, thinly sliced

2 (15-ounce) cans no-salt-added **cannellini beans** or other **white beans**, rinsed and drained

4 sprigs **fresh rosemary** (optional)

Remove the stems from the chard and dice them. Coarsely chop the leaves.

Put ½ cup of the broth in a medium saucepan and bring to a boil over medium-high heat. Add the garlic and chard stems. Cook, stirring frequently, until the broth has been absorbed and the vegetables are beginning to stick, 3 to 5 minutes. Add the remaining broth and bring to a boil. Add the chard leaves and stir. Return the mixture to a boil, then decrease the heat to maintain a simmer. Cook, stirring occasionally, until the vegetables are tender, 15 to 20 minutes. Add the beans and the optional rosemary sprigs and stir. Increase the heat to medium-high and return to a simmer. Decrease the heat to medium-low and cook, stirring frequently, until the liquid has reduced to a sauce, about 5 minutes. Remove the rosemary sprigs and discard. Serve immediately.

Black-Eyed Peas with Kale

Curly kale is surprisingly meaty, chewy, and satiating. When paired with black-eyed peas, the protein is elevated and the satisfaction level is unbeatable.

1 **onion**, diced

½ **red bell pepper**, diced

1 stalk **celery**, diced

4 cloves **garlic**, minced or pressed

1 large bunch **curly kale**, ribs removed and leaves coarsely chopped

½ teaspoon **hot smoked paprika** or **smoked paprika** plus a pinch of **cayenne**

1½ cups unsalted **vegetable broth**

¾ cup no-salt-added **tomato purée**

2 (15-ounce) cans no-salt-added **black-eyed peas**, rinsed and drained

1 sprig **fresh thyme**, or ½ teaspoon **dried thyme**

Mist a medium saucepan with olive oil spray and place over medium-low heat. When hot, add the onion, bell pepper, celery, and garlic. Cover and cook, stirring frequently, until nearly dry, about 10 minutes. Add the kale and stir until wilted, about 2 minutes. Add the smoked paprika and stir to combine. Add the broth and tomato purée and stir thoroughly. Cook until the kale is tender and the liquid has reduced to a sauce, about 15 minutes.

Stir in the black-eyed peas and thyme. Cook, stirring occasionally, until the aroma of thyme arises. Remove the thyme sprig, if using. Serve immediately.

Tempeh Chili

Protein-rich tempeh is a great replacement for ground beef in this otherwise very traditional chili.

8 ounces plain **tempeh**

1 **red onion**, diced

3 cloves **garlic**, minced or pressed

1 (14-ounce) can chopped **tomatoes**

3 tablespoons **chili spice blend**

2 tablespoons **white corn masa harina** (optional; see tip)

1 (15-ounce) can no-salt-added **red beans**, rinsed and drained

8 **scallions**, thinly sliced (optional)

Break the tempeh into 4 or 5 pieces and put in a food processor. Pulse until the tempeh is chopped and has the texture of a very coarse meal.

Mist a 2-quart saucepan with olive oil spray and place over medium heat. Add the onion and garlic and cook, stirring constantly, until softened, about 5 minutes. Add the tempeh and cook, stirring constantly, until it begins to stick, 2 to 3 minutes. Add the tomatoes and stir to loosen any bits that may have stuck to the saucepan. Add the chili spice blend and bring to a boil, stirring constantly. Decrease the heat to maintain a simmer. Cover and cook, stirring occasionally, for 10 minutes.

Put the optional masa harina in a small bowl. Add ¼ cup cold water and stir to combine. Continue stirring until a watery paste forms. Add to the chili and stir until thoroughly combined. Cook until the mixture thickens slightly, about 2 minutes. Add the beans and stir until warmed through.

Divide the chili among four bowls and garnish with the optional scallions. Serve immediately.

> TIP Masa harina contributes significantly to the overall flavor of chili, but it also serves as a thickener, binding the other components together. It is available at most supermarkets in the Mexican food or "international" section.

Black Bean and Vegetable Stew

Bean and vegetable stews are mainstays, and this one is great to add to your weekly rotation. Loaded with antioxidant and anti-inflammatory vegetables, it's quite easy to prepare and the cooking time is only about thirty minutes, although it tastes like it simmered all day.

2 stalks **celery**

1 large **onion**, diced

2 **carrots**, diced

1 **red bell pepper**, diced

2 **zucchini**, diced

4 cloves **garlic**, thinly sliced

1 tablespoon **smoked paprika**

½ cup no-salt-added **tomato purée**

4 cups unsalted **vegetable broth**

1 cup fresh or canned **corn kernels**

2 (15-ounce) cans no-salt-added **black beans**, undrained

½ cup coarsely chopped **cilantro**, lightly packed (optional)

Peel the celery to remove the strings. Dice the celery.

Place a large saucepan over medium-high heat. When hot, mist the saucepan with olive oil spray. Add the onion and stir until it begins to soften, about 3 minutes. Add the celery, carrots, and bell pepper. Cook, stirring constantly, until the vegetables begin to release their juices, about 3 minutes. Add the zucchini and garlic and continue cooking, stirring frequently, until the garlic releases its aroma, about 2 minutes. Add the smoked paprika and stir to coat the vegetables. Add the tomato purée, broth, and corn. Bring to a simmer and cook, stirring occasionally, until all the vegetables are tender and the liquid has reduced to a sauce, about 20 minutes.

Add the black beans and their liquid and stir to mix thoroughly. Reheat until barely simmering. Remove from the heat and stir in the optional cilantro. Serve immediately.

Stuffed Acorn Squash

Acorn squash is meaty and colorful. When halved and stuffed, it makes a gorgeous centerpiece for a special occasion dinner or holiday feast.

2 **acorn squashes**

6 tablespoons unsalted **vegetable broth**

Freshly ground **black pepper**

1 **red onion**, diced

2 stalks **celery**, diced

1 **pear** or **apple**, diced

½ cup **apple juice**

2 cups cooked **red** or **white quinoa**

1 cup **pecans**, coarsely chopped

¼ cup chopped **fresh parsley**, lightly packed

Preheat the oven to 375 degrees F.

Cut the squashes in half lengthwise and scoop out the seeds. Put them in a baking dish, cut-side up. Pour 1 tablespoon of the broth into the cavity of each half and season lightly with pepper. Cover the squashes with a sheet of parchment paper or foil to keep them moist. Bake for 1 hour, or until tender. Decrease the oven temperature to 300 degrees F.

Put the remaining 2 tablespoons of broth in a medium saucepan over medium-high heat. Add the onion and celery and cook, stirring almost constantly, until the broth has been absorbed, about 4 minutes. Add the pear and cook until the pear and vegetables are beginning to brown, about 3 minutes. Add the apple juice and stir. Add the quinoa and half the pecans and parsley. Stir until the quinoa is warmed through. Remove from the heat.

Divide the filling equally among the four squash halves, mounding it gently. Return the squashes to the oven and bake for 15 minutes, or until heated through. Garnish with the remaining pecans and parsley and serve immediately.

Red Quinoa–Stuffed Mushrooms

Red quinoa has a rich, dark color, which is often found in foods high in anti-inflammatory and antioxidant compounds. Who knew that a healthy whole grain could be so beautiful, tasty, and satisfying!

1 cup **red quinoa**

2 cups unsalted **vegetable broth**

1 small **red onion**, minced

1 small stalk **celery**, minced

½ **roasted red pepper**, minced

2 teaspoons **herbes de Provence**, **fines herbes**, or other **herb blend**

4 large **portobello mushrooms**

Freshly ground **black pepper**

½ cup chopped **parsley**, lightly packed

½ cup **pecans**, lightly toasted and coarsely chopped

Put the quinoa in a small saucepan. Add the broth and bring to a boil over medium-high heat. Decrease the heat to low, cover, and cook for 20 minutes. If any liquid remains, continue cooking until it has been absorbed, up to 10 minutes longer, checking occasionally. Remove from the heat.

Preheat the oven to 400 degrees F.

Place a medium saucepan over medium-high heat. When hot, mist with olive oil spray and add the onion and celery. Decrease the heat to medium and cook, stirring frequently, until the vegetables just begin to stick, 7 to 9 minutes. Add the roasted red pepper, herbes de Provence, and the cooked quinoa. Cook, stirring occasionally, until warmed through, 2 to 3 minutes. Cover and remove from the heat.

Remove the stems from the mushrooms and season the caps with pepper. Place a large ovenproof skillet over medium-high heat. When hot, mist with olive oil spray and add the mushrooms, gills down. Cook until lightly browned, 3 to 4 minutes. Turn the mushrooms over and remove the skillet from the heat.

Set aside 2 teaspoons of the parsley and add the remainder to the quinoa mixture along with the pecans. Stir to incorporate. Divide the quinoa among the mushrooms, mounding it, spreading it to the edges, and pressing down gently. Mist the tops with olive oil spray. Transfer the skillet to the oven and bake for 15 minutes, or until hot and the filling is lightly browned. Garnish the tops with the remaining parsley and serve immediately.

Cherry Sorbet

Rich in anthocyanins, cherries are extremely high on the anti-inflammatory scale.

- 4 cups frozen **cherries**
- ¾ cup unsweetened **apple juice**
- 9 pitted medjool **dates**
- 2 teaspoons **vanilla extract**

Put all the ingredients in a high-speed blender and process, using the plunger, until smooth and creamy, stopping occasionally to scrape down the sides of the container as needed. Transfer to a 1-quart container and freeze until firm, 8 to 12 hours. To freeze more quickly, spread in the bottom of a metal loaf pan and freeze for 3 to 4 hours before serving.

Strawberry Ice Cream

No ice-cream maker is needed for this naturally sweet banana-based ice cream.

3 frozen ripe **bananas**, broken into chunks

1 cup frozen **strawberries**

¼ cup unsweetened **soymilk** or **almond milk**

1 tablespoon **Date Paste** (optional)

½ teaspoon **vanilla extract**

Put all the ingredients in a high-speed blender and process, using the plunger, until smooth and creamy, stopping occasionally to scrape down the sides of the container as needed. Spread in the bottom of a metal loaf pan and put in the freezer for at least 2 hours before serving.

TIP A high-speed blender (such as a Vitamix) is essential for making banana-based ice cream. Please don't attempt this recipe in a standard blender. For the perfect presentation, use an ice-cream scoop to dish it out.

Mocha Ice Cream

Use decaf coffee in this recipe if you prefer.

3 frozen large ripe **bananas**, broken into pieces

½ cup cold brewed **coffee**

¼ cup unsweetened **cocoa powder**

1 teaspoon **vanilla extract**

Pinch **sea salt**

⅓ cup coarsely chopped **dark chocolate** (optional)

Put the bananas, coffee, cocoa powder, vanilla extract, and sea salt in a high-speed blender and process, using the plunger, until smooth and creamy, stopping occasionally to scrape down the sides of the container as needed. Stir or pulse in the optional chopped chocolate. Spread in the bottom of a metal loaf pan and put in the freezer for at least 2 hours before serving.

TIP A high-speed blender (such as a Vitamix) is essential for making banana-based ice cream. Please don't attempt this recipe in a standard blender. For the perfect presentation, use an ice-cream scoop to dish it out.

Chocolate Ice Cream

This banana-based treat tastes exactly like its dairy counterpart. No one will know this luscious dessert is a health food in disguise!

3 frozen ripe **bananas**, broken into chunks

3 tablespoons unsweetened **cocoa powder**

1½ tablespoons unsweetened, no-salt-added smooth **almond butter** or **peanut butter**

2 tablespoons unsweetened **soymilk** or **almond milk**

Put all the ingredients in a high-speed blender and process, using the plunger, until smooth and creamy, stopping occasionally to scrape down the sides of the container as needed. Spread in the bottom of a metal loaf pan and put in the freezer for at least 2 hours before serving.

> TIP A high-speed blender (such as a Vitamix) is essential for making banana-based ice cream. Please don't attempt this recipe in a standard blender. For the perfect presentation, use an ice-cream scoop to dish it out.

Mint Chocolate Chip Ice Cream

Incredibly refreshing, this winning banana-based ice cream is especially gratifying in warmer weather.

3 frozen ripe **bananas**, broken into chunks

¼ cup **baby spinach** (optional)

2 tablespoons unsweetened **soymilk** or **almond milk**

½ teaspoon **peppermint extract**

3 tablespoons **dark chocolate chips**

Put bananas, optional spinach, soymilk, and peppermint extract in a high-speed blender and process, using the plunger, until smooth and creamy, stopping occasionally to scrape down the sides of the container as needed. Pulse in the chocolate chips, just until they are coarsely chopped. Spread in the bottom of a metal loaf pan and put in the freezer for at least 2 hours before serving.

> TIP A high-speed blender (such as a Vitamix) is essential for making banana-based ice cream. Please don't attempt this recipe in a standard blender. For the perfect presentation, use an ice-cream scoop to dish it out.
>
> The spinach can't be tasted in the ice cream, but it will add the lovely green hue that is commonly associated with mint ice cream.

Baked Apples

Although sweet treats should be limited, this dish contains no added sugar, as its sweetness is derived naturally from fruits. This good-for-you dessert looks as special as it tastes, and since it's health-supporting, you can serve it without hesitation to family, friends, and guests.

4 ripe **Fuji** or other **semisweet apples**

¼ cup **Date Paste** (page 127)

1 teaspoon **vanilla bean paste** or **vanilla extract**

½ teaspoon **ground cinnamon**

¼ teaspoon **ground cloves**

¼ teaspoon **ground allspice**

½ cup **pecans**, coarsely chopped

¼ cup **dark rum**

Preheat the oven to 350 degrees F.

Core the apples. Combine the Date Paste, vanilla bean paste, cinnamon, cloves, allspice and half the pecans in a small bowl and stir until well combined. Divide the paste among the apples, stuffing it into the cavities. Put the apples in a small baking dish, fitting them as tightly as possible in order to keep them upright. Divide the remaining pecans among the apples, piling them on the tops. Sprinkle the rum over the apples.

Cover the baking dish with foil and bake the apples for 40 minutes. Uncover and spoon any accumulated juices over the tops. Continue baking, uncovered, for 15 to 20 minutes longer, until the tops are browned and a skewer inserted from the side meets no resistance. Serve immediately.

Sautéed Apricots WITH AMARETTO AND CASHEW CREAM

Decadently delicious, this enchanting dessert is an excellent choice for any special occasion or celebration.

2 teaspoons **Date Paste** (page 127)

¼ teaspoon **vanilla bean paste**, or 1 teaspoon **vanilla extract**

12 **apricots**, quartered, or 4 **nectarines** or **peaches**, cubed

2 tablespoons **Amaretto**, or ½ teaspoon **almond extract**

1 cup **Cashew Dessert Cream** (page 159), without the optional cardamom

Put the Date Paste and vanilla bean paste in a small bowl and stir to combine. Add 1 tablespoon of water and stir until smooth.

Place a sauté pan over high heat until hot. Mist with olive oil spray and add the apricots. Shake the pan briskly to toss the apricots until they just begin to soften, about 2 minutes. Add the Date Paste mixture and swirl the pan briskly to coat the apricots. Add the Amaretto and swirl for 10 seconds. Divide among four small bowls. Divide the Cashew Dessert Cream among the bowls, placing a dollop on top of the apricots. Serve immediately!

> TIP If you have a gas stove, be sure to lean back when you add the Amaretto, as it may suddenly ignite.

Cashew Dessert Cream

So luscious over fresh berries or sliced or cubed seasonal fruits, this dairy-free cream makes the ordinary taste extraordinary.

½ cup raw **cashews**

⅔ cup **water**

1 tablespoon **Date Paste** (page 127)

1 teaspoon **vanilla extract**

Pinch **ground cardamom**, **ground cinnamon**, or **ground cloves** (optional)

Put the cashews in a small heatproof bowl. Cover with boiling water and let sit until cooled. Drain the cashews, rinse, and drain again.

Put the cashews, water, Date Paste, and vanilla extract in a blender and process until smooth. Transfer to a bowl or jar. Stir in the optional cardamom. Serve immediately or chill in the refrigerator before serving. Stored in a sealed container in the refrigerator, the cream will keep for about three days.

Monica Aggarwal, MD, is an associate professor of medicine at the University of Florida Division of Cardiovascular Medicine, where she also serves as the director of integrative cardiology and prevention. In addition, she is the director of medical education for cardiology, where she oversees the education of medical residents and cardiology fellows, with a focus on prevention, nutrition, and lifestyle. She is board certified in cardiology, echocardiography, advanced lipids, and nuclear cardiology. For more information, visit drmonicaaggarwal.com.

Jyothi Rao, MD, has worked in clinical practice since 1997. She is board certified in internal medicine and antiaging and regenerative medicine. Dr. Rao is currently the medical director of the Shakthi Health and Wellness Center, a hub for integrative medicine that focuses on supporting the relationship between the mind and body for enhanced vitality and whole-body wellness. Her website is raowellness.com.

books that educate, inspire, and empower

To find your favorite books on plant-based cooking and nutrition,
raw-foods cuisine, and healthy living, visit:

BookPubCo.com

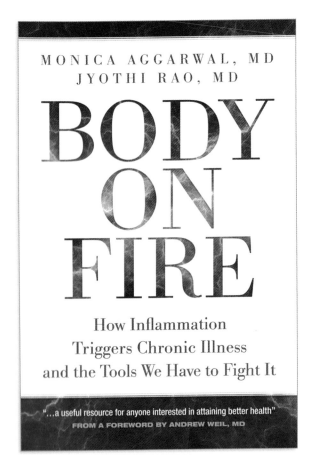

Numerous lifestyle factors can lead to inflammation, which in turn can trigger a number of illnesses. Drs. Monica Aggarwal and Jyothi Rao help readers take an honest assessment of their energy, lifestyle, dietary habits, and mental state and provide a series of interventions for reclaiming health.

In-depth explanations of the dangers of stress and the benefits of microbiomes on not only digestive health but also general well-being show how common dietary and lifestyle changes can make a dynamic difference.

BODY ON FIRE
How Inflammation Triggers Chronic Illness and the Tools We Have to Fight It

Monica Aggarwal, MD & Jyothi Rao, MD

Print: 978-1-57067-392-4
$19.95 • 256 pages • trade paper • 6 x 9
E-book: 978-1-57067-828-8
Unabridged Audio Book: 9781570674051
7 hours 18 minutes

Purchase these titles from your favorite book source or buy them directly from:
BPC • PO Box 99 • Summertown, TN 38483 • 1-888-260-8458

Free shipping and handling on all orders